The Civil War
A Book of Quotations

Edited by
Bob Blaisdell

DOVER PUBLICATIONS, INC.
Mineola, New York

Dedication

To my father

—B.B.

Copyright

Copyright © 2004 by Dover Publications, Inc.
All rights reserved.

Bibliographical Note

The Civil War: A Book of Quotations is a new work, first published by Dover Publications, Inc., in 2004.

Library of Congress Cataloging-in-Publication Data

The Civil War : a book of quotations / edited by Bob Blaisdell.
    p. cm.
    Includes index.
    ISBN 0-486-43413-3 (pbk.)
    1. United States—History—Civil War, 1861–1865—Quotations, maxims, etc. 2. Quotations, American. I. Blaisdell, Robert.

E468.9.C47 2004
973.7—dc22

2004041348

Manufactured in the United States of America
Dover Publications, Inc., 31 East 2nd Street, Mineola, N.Y. 11501

Note

These hundreds of quotes can engage us with the voices, strident and brave, blustery and violent, spontaneous and reflective, of the worst and yet most important war of United States history. These are the voices of the war's presidents, Abraham Lincoln and Jefferson Davis, its leading generals, Ulysses S. Grant and Robert E. Lee, as well as of dozens of other officers, soldiers, politicians, and families on both sides.

I have provided brief contextual notes for particular quotes and sections to remind or inform readers of the various situations. My ambitions for this book were, I confess, for it to provide its own self-contained narrative, but I have realized no single book can do that for this gigantic, uncontainable topic, no matter the length. To *begin* to appreciate the grand and terrible story of the Civil War, however, I recommend Shelby Foote's great *The Civil War: A Narrative* and James M. McPherson's *Battle Cry of Freedom*; for a *contemporary*, running account of the war, I have found nothing can beat Frank Moore's *Rebellion Record*, in ten volumes (1861–1867), which traces the war day by day, at home and on the field, with official documents, newspaper reports, and anecdotal and poetic accounts. Foote's and Moore's volumes have provided me with many of the quotations, with other volumes also being extremely useful, including the unwieldy *War of the Rebellion: Official Records,* Henry Steele Commager's *The Blue and the Gray,* Bell Irvin Wiley's wonderful *The Life of Johnny Reb* and *The Life of Billy Yank,* Richard B. Harwell's *The Union Reader* and *The Confederate Reader,* E. B. Long's *The Civil War Day by Day,* and Harold Holzer's first-rate *Witness to War.*

My father, Dr. F. William Blaisdell, a lifelong Civil War enthusiast, has made a variety of suggestions to help me find materials, clarify the notes, and arrange the quotations. He has provided the majority of the quotations on Civil War medicine, one
of his particular interests.

Each quotation in this book has a lettered code in square
brackets that is keyed to the list of sources on page 178.

Contents

THE CIVIL WAR
A Book of Quotations

The roots of the Civil War antedated the United States, and, said one American politician in the 1850s, went as far back as Satan. Despite efforts to do so, the Founding Fathers, in composing and ratifying the Constitution in 1787, were unable to eradicate slavery from the new country. They knew that some day their descendants would have to confront a regionally divisive moral issue. Even while Southerners argued for states' rights, the balance of power between North and South, and the right to decide for themselves their own customs, the South's most conspicuous and distinctive custom was slavery. "The question of Negro slavery has been the apple of discord in the government of the United States since its foundation," said Alabama lawyer Robert H. Smith, shortly after he had helped compose the Confederate Constitution. Ulysses S. Grant, the great Union general who spearheaded the North's victory in the Civil War, ruefully reflected in 1885, twenty years after the war's conclusion: "For the present, and so long as there are living witnesses of the great war of sections, there will be people who will not be consoled for the loss of a cause which they believed to be holy. As time passes, people, even of the South, will begin to wonder how it was possible that their ancestors ever fought for or justified institutions which acknowledged the right of property in man."

The decade before the war saw the abolitionist movement gain terrific power in the North, a movement perhaps personified more for its enemies than for its adherents by John Brown, who believed the violence of slavery needed to be fought with violence. In reaction to more peaceful and moderate abolitionists, politicians from the South argued the constitutional validity of secession. Why didn't a state have the right to secede? Were the states in existence for the sake of the country, or was the United States a country for the states? Abolition or secession, a dramatic change was coming, one way or the other. Rather than submit to the inevitable democratic processes and social progress, South Carolina's most vocal representatives, prominent for their slaveholding interests, drew a line in the sand in 1860, announcing the state's intention of seceding if the Republican candidate for the presidency, Abraham Lincoln, won the election.

Pre-War to 1861

The quotations in this section are a sampling of the most divisive and resonant that led to the outbreak of secession.

It is a truth of history, untouched by an exception, that no nation has ever yet matured its political growth without the stern and scarring experience of civil war. . . . But, while prepared for any consequence, where is the probability of civil war resulting from Southern secession? In the first place, what motive would influence the North to an invasive war? If there be any truth in protests of our Northern brethren—if slavery be a burden to their consciences, why interfere against an Exodus which would carry with it the plague—why not let the South and slavery go together?
    —William Henry Trescot, secessionist, Charleston, South Carolina, from his pamphlet, "The Position and Course of the South," 1850 [SPS, 28: ref: Charleston: Walker and James, 1850]

Near eighty years ago we began by declaring that all men are created equal; but now from that beginning we have run down to the other declaration, that for some men to enslave others is a "sacred right of self-government." These principles cannot stand together.
    —Abraham Lincoln, lawyer and former congressman, speech at Peoria, Illinois, October 16, 1854
    [BCF]

❖❖❖

It is not alone a fight between the North and the South; it is a fight between freedom and slavery; between God and the devil; between heaven and hell.

—George Washington Julian, of Indiana, a founder of the Free Soil Party and a future Republican congressman, speech, October 21, 1856
[WW]

I believe this government cannot endure, permanently half *slave* and half *free*. I do not expect the Union to be *dissolved*— I do not expect the house to *fall*—but I *do* expect it will cease to be divided. It will become *all* one thing or *all* the other.

—Abraham Lincoln, acceptance speech for the nomination for U.S. senator, Republican State Convention, Springfield, Illinois, June 16, 1858
[GS]

Shall I tell you what this collision means? They who think that it is accidental, unnecessary, the work of interested or fanatical agitators, and therefore ephemeral, mistake the case altogether. It is an irrepressible conflict between opposing and enduring forces, and it means the United States must and will, sooner or later, become either entirely a slave-holding nation or entirely a free-labor nation. . . . I know, and you know, that a revolution has begun.

—U.S. Senator William H. Seward, Republican from New York, speech at Rochester, New York, October 25, 1858. (Seward became Lincoln's secretary of state, and was nearly killed in the assassination conspiracy that did kill President Lincoln in 1865.)
[WW]

Talk! talk! talk! That will never free the slaves. What is needed is action—action.

—John Brown, abolitionist, having attended a New England Anti-Slavery Society meeting, spring 1859
[BCF]

❖❖❖

These ministers who profess to be Christian, and hold slaves or advocate slavery, I cannot abide them. My knees will not bend in prayer with them, while their hands are stained with the blood of souls.

—John Brown, letter to Reverend McFarland, from jail in Virginia, November 23, 1859. (After leading violent raids on slaveholders, Brown captured the federal armory at Harper's Ferry, Virginia, on October 16, 1859, in preparation, he hoped, for leading a slave revolt. He was captured on October 18, 1859, by U.S. Marines led by Colonel Robert E. Lee and Lieutenant J. E. B. Stuart, who would become important Confederate generals.)
[JB]

I John Brown am now quite *certain* that the crimes of this *guilty land;* will never be purged away; but with blood.

—John Brown, note found after his execution by hanging, Charlestown, Virginia, December 2, 1859
[CW-1]

The whole country is in a state of fearful agitation—disunion! disunion! is the cry with our Southern friends; it is boldly spoken of by the fireside, in public, in all places it is the absorbing subject. The aggressions of the North and the insults to which we are subjected in their papers, their treasonable acts, how can it be otherwise if our rights as guaranteed by the Constitution are trampled under foot defiantly—disunion must follow. Southern men and women will not sit down with folded hands if the masses elect a Black Republican President.

—Southern woman, letter to her son, January 11, 1860
[EL, 134: ref: Kirby Smith Papers, University of North Carolina]

The fact that we get no votes in your section, is a fact of your making, and not of ours. And if there be fault in that fact, that fault is primarily yours, and remains until you show that we repel you by some wrong principle or practice.

—Abraham Lincoln, Republican Party, speech, "a few words to the Southern people," at the Cooper Institute, New York City, February 27, 1860
[GS]

❖❖❖

I hold that the election of any man on earth by the American people, according to the Constitution, is no justification for breaking up this government.

—Presidential candidate Stephen Douglas, having realized that Abraham Lincoln would win the election, went to Tennessee, Georgia, and Alabama, in an attempt to avert their secession, November 1860
[BCF]

I glory in Mississippi's star! But before I would see it dishonored I would tear it from its place, to be set on the perilous ridge of battle as a sign around which her bravest and best shall meet the harvest home of death.

—U.S. Senator Jefferson Davis of Mississippi, in Mississippi, November 5, 1860. (Davis had served as the secretary of war under President Franklin Pierce in 1853, and would become the president of the Confederacy.)
[CW-1]

Ain't you glad you joined the Republicans?
Joined the Republicans,
Ain't you glad you joined the Republicans,
Down in Illinois?

—Female chorus at the Watson Saloon, Springfield, Illinois, singing to the newly elected president, Abraham Lincoln, November 6, 1860
[CWDD, 3]

If the Cotton States shall become satisfied that they can do better out of the Union than in it, we insist on letting them go. We hope never to live in a republic whereof one section is pinned to the residue by bayonets.

—Horace Greeley, editor of the *New York Tribune*, editorial, November 9, 1860
[BCF]

❖❖❖

I think I see in the future a gory head rise above our horizon. Its name is Civil War. Already I can see the prints of his bloody fingers upon our lintels and doorposts. The vision sickens me already.
—Thomas Reade Rootes Cobb, Georgian pro-secessionist leader, speech in Milledgeville, Georgia, November 12, 1860. (He served as a general in the Confederate army and was killed at Fredericksburg, December 13, 1862.)
[WW]

The long-continued and intemperate interference of the Northern people with the question of slavery in the Southern States has at length produced its natural effects.
—President James Buchanan, State of the Union address to Congress, Washington, D.C., December 4, 1860. (In the same address, however, the president also scolded the South: "Secession is neither more nor less than revolution.")
[CWDD, 8]

Let there be no compromise on the question of extending slavery. If there is, all our labor is lost, and, ere long, must be done again. The dangerous ground—that into which some of our friends have a hankering to run—is Popular Sovereignty. Have none of it. Stand firm. The tug has to come, and better now, than at any time hereafter.
—President-elect Abraham Lincoln, letter to friend Senator Lyman Trumbull, December 10, 1860
[CF, 166]

The sole cause of the existing disunion excitement which is about to break up the government is the war which has been carried on for years past all manner of devices by the antislavery fanatical sentiment upon more than $2,000,000,000 of property.
—U.S. Senator James A. Bayard of Delaware, letter to his son, December 12, 1860
[EL, 331: ref: Bayard Papers]

Secession is not intended to break up the present Government, but to perpetuate it. We do not propose to go out by way of

❖❖❖

breaking up or destroying the Union as our fathers gave it to us, but we go out for the purpose of getting further guaranties and security for our rights.

—A. H. Handy, Commissioner of Mississippi, address to the citizens of Baltimore, Maryland, December 19, 1860
[RR 1, Diary, 3]

If the general government should persist in the measures now threatened, there must be *war.* It is painful to discover with what unconcern they speak of war, and threaten it. They do not know its horrors. I have seen enough of it to make me look upon it as the sum of all evils.

—Thomas J. (not yet "Stonewall") Jackson, professor of Natural Philosophy at Virginia Military Institute, to his pastor, Reverend William White, Lexington, Virginia, December 19, 1860
[TJJ]

. . . the union now subsisting between South Carolina and other States, under the name of "The United States of America," is hereby dissolved.

—"We, the People of the State of South Carolina, in Convention assembled," ordinance, December 20, 1860. (South Carolina was the first of eleven states to secede.)
[CR]

They have this day set a blazing torch to the temple of constitutional liberty and, please God, we shall have no more peace forever.

—Judge James Petigru, of South Carolina, an opponent of the state's secession, December 20, 1860
[CF, 133]

Secession by the 4th day of March should be thundered from the ballot-box by the unanimous vote of Georgia on the 2nd day of January next. Such a voice will be your best guarantee for liberty, security, tranquillity, and glory.

—Robert Toombs, address "to the people of Georgia," from Washington, D.C., December 24, 1860
[RR 1, Doc, 8]

❖❖❖

The election of Mr. Lincoln, I am well persuaded, is owing much more to the divisions of the Democratic party, and the disastrous personal strifes among its leaders . . . than to any fixed determination on the part of a majority of the people of the North to wage an exterminating war against Southern institutions.
   —Alexander H. Stephens of Georgia, who would become vice president of the Confederacy, letter, December 24, 1860
   [RR 1, Diary, 28]

You people of the South don't know what you are doing. This country will be drenched in blood, and God only knows how it will end. It is all folly, madness, a crime against civilization! You people speak so lightly of war; you don't know what you're talking about. War is a terrible thing! . . . You are rushing into war with one of the most powerful, ingeniously mechanical and determined people on earth—right at your doors.
   —William Tecumseh Sherman, of Ohio, while superintendent of the Louisiana State Military Academy, in Baton Rouge, in discussion with Professor David F. Boyd, from Virginia, December 24, 1860. (Sherman quit the school before Louisiana seceded, went north, and became one of the Union's greatest generals.)
   [CW-1]

The only question is: can we reconstruct any government without bloodshed? I do not think we can—a few old political hacks and barroom bullies are leading public opinion. . . . They can easily pull down a government, but when another is to be built, who will confide in them? Yet no one seems to reflect that anything more is necessary than to secede.
   —Braxton Bragg, letter to his friend, William Tecumseh Sherman, late December 1860. (Bragg, a Virginian living in Louisiana, became a major general in the Confederate army.)
   [CWY, 20]

So long as the United States keeps possession of this fort [Fort Sumter], the independence of South Carolina will only be in name, not in fact. If, however, it should be surrendered to South

Carolina, which I do not apprehend, *the smothered indignation of the free states would be roused beyond control.*
—General John Wool, letter from Troy, New York, to a friend in Washington, D.C., December 31, 1860. (By this time South Carolina had seized all federal property within its borders except Fort Sumter.)
[RR 1, Doc, 10]

What may be the fate of this horrible contest, no man can tell, none pretend to foresee; but this much I will say: the fortunes of war may be adverse to our arms; you may carry desolation into our peaceful land, and with torch and fire you may set our cities in flames; . . . you may do all this—and more, too, if more there be—but you never can subjugate us; you never can convert the free sons of the soil into vassals, paying tribute to your power; and you never, never can degrade them to the level of an inferior and servile race. Never! Never!
—U.S. Senator Judah P. Benjamin of Louisiana, speech to the Senate, Washington, D.C., December 31, 1860. (Benjamin resigned from the Senate in February and served as secretary of war and secretary of state in the Confederacy.)
[SPS, 114]

———— ❖❖❖ ————

1861

Would there be a war, and if so, what would "war" mean? By February 1, Mississippi, Florida, Alabama, Louisiana, Georgia, and Texas had seceded. The seceding states quickly took over whatever federal arsenals and property they could. Meanwhile, President Buchanan did little to prevent such seizures, and President-elect Lincoln, slowly crossing the country in February, said little about the crisis. On February 9, the Confederacy named Jefferson Davis its provisional president. Davis, who had been eager to serve as a general, reluctantly accepted. The original Confederate capital was in Montgomery, Alabama. After Virginia seceded in April, the capital moved to Richmond. Arkansas, North Carolina, and Tennessee seceded in May and June.

✿

SECESSION CONTINUES

I do not know what the Union would be worth if saved by the use of the sword.
— U.S. Senator William Henry Seward of New York, speech in the Senate, January 12, 1861
[CWDD, 26]

Suppose these slaves were liberated: suppose the people of the South would today voluntarily consent to surrender $3,000,000,000 of slave property, and send their slaves at their expense into the free States, would you accept them as freemen and citizens in your States? You dare not answer me that you would. You would fight us with all the energy and power of your

States for twenty years, before you would submit to it. And yet you demand of us to liberate them, to surrender this $3,000,000,000 of slave property, to dissolve society, to break up social-order, to ruin our commercial and political prospects for the future, and still to retain such an element among us.

—U.S. Representative John H. Reagan of Texas, speech to the House of Representatives, January 15, 1861. (After resigning from the House of Representatives, Reagan served as the Confederacy's post-master general.)
[SPS, 143: ref: Washington, D.C.: W. H. Moore, 1861]

This step, secession, once taken, can never be recalled. We and our posterity shall see our lovely South desolated by the demon of war.

—Alexander H. Stephens, of Georgia, the day before the State Convention of Georgia adopted the secession ordinance, January 18, 1861
[RR 1, 208]

May God have us in His holy keeping, and grant that before it is too late, peaceful councils may prevail.

—U.S. Senator Jefferson Davis of Mississippi, overheard talking to himself by Varina Davis, his wife, the night of the day he resigned from the Senate, January 21, 1861. (Mississippi had seceded on January 9.)
[CW-1]

You may, after the sacrifice of countless millions of treasure and hundreds of thousands of lives, as a bare possibility, win Southern independence. . . . But I doubt it. I tell you that, while I believe with you in the doctrine of States Rights, the North is determined to preserve this Union. They are not a fiery, impulsive people as you are, for they live in colder climates. But when they begin to move in a given direction . . . they move with the steady momentum and perseverance of a mighty avalanche.

—Sam Houston, governor of Texas, speech to the Texas legislature, which was inclining toward secession, January 1861. (Texas seceded February 1. On March 18, Houston refused to swear allegiance to the Confederacy, and was officially deposed as governor.)
[SH, 409]

❖❖❖

The framers of our Constitution never exhausted so much labor, wisdom, and forbearance in its formation, if it was intended to be broken up by every member of the [Union] at will. . . . It is idle to talk of secession.
—U.S. Marine Colonel Robert E. Lee, January 1861. (In April, when his home state of Virginia seceded, Lee resigned from the federal service and accepted a generalship with the Confederacy.) [BCF]

If Captain Breshwood, after arrest, undertakes to interfere with the command of the cutter, tell Lieutenant Caldwell to consider him a mutineer, and treat him accordingly. If anyone attempts to haul down the American flag, shoot him on the spot.
—Secretary of the Treasury John Dix, letter to W. H. Jones, Special Agent of the Treasury, New Orleans, after Captain Breshwood, of a Treasury cutter, "refused positively in writing, to obey any instructions," according to Jones, January 29, 1861. (Breshwood turned the ship over to the state of Louisiana, not the Treasury Department, on this date.) [RR 1]

The separation is perfect, complete, and perpetual. The great duty is now imposed upon us of providing for those States a government for their future security and protection.
—Howell Cobb of Georgia, addressing the Convention of Seceded States, Montgomery, Alabama, the first session of the Provisional Congress of the Confederate States of America, February 4, 1861 [CWDD, 30]

First, gallant South Carolina nobly made the stand;
Then came Alabama, who took her by the hand;
Next, quickly Mississippi, Georgia and Florida,
All raised on high the Bonnie Blue Flag that bears
    a single star.

We are a band of brothers, and natives to the soil,
Fighting for the property we gained by honest toil;

❖❖❖

And when our rights were threatened, the cry rose
    near and far:
Hurrah for the bonnie Blue Flag that bears the single star!
    —"The Bonnie Blue Flag," by Harry McCarthy, of New Orleans, on
    the order of secession, 1861. (Louisiana, Texas, Virginia, Arkansas,
    North Carolina, and then Tennessee followed the above states.)
    [RR 4, Poetry, 84]

The people of Virginia recognize the American principle, that
government is founded in the consent of the governed, and the
right of the people of the several States of the Union, for just
cause, to withdraw from their association under the Federal
government, with the people of the other States, and to erect
new government for their better security; and they never will
consent that the Federal power, which is, in part, their power,
shall be exerted for the purpose of subjugating the people of
such States to the Federal authority.
    —Sovereign Convention of Virginia, February 4, 1861
    [SHW, 68]

The institution of slavery is doing more in the agency of the
world's great progress, more for the improvement and comfort
of human life, more for the preaching of the Gospel to heathen
nations, more for the fulfillment of prophecy, than any other
institution on earth.
    —Florida Governor Richard K. Call, letter to John S. Littell of
    Pennsylvania, February 12, 1861
    [RR 1, 265]

Slavery cannot share a government with democracy.
    —L. W. Spratt, of South Carolina, letter to John Perkins of
    Louisiana, who was helping form the Confederate Constitution,
    February 13, 1861. (Spratt protested the prohibition of the slave
    trade outside of North America, and argued for the acknowledg-
    ment that the Confederacy would be a "Slave Republic," as it could
    not exist as a democracy, which he believed was a system of gov-
    ernment that would *inevitably* abolish slavery.)
    [RR 2, Doc, 365]

❖❖❖

It is true that while I hold myself without mock modesty the humblest of all individuals that have ever been elevated to the Presidency, I have a more difficult task to perform than any one of them.
—President-elect Abraham Lincoln, speech to the New York State Legislature, Albany, New York, February 18, 1861
[CWDD, 39]

If an old woman with a broomstick should come with full authority from the state of Texas to demand the public property, I would give it to her.
—Major General David E. Twiggs, commander of the Department of Texas, February 18, 1861. (Twiggs obligingly surrendered the federal military stores and forces to a representative of the state of Texas, and was dismissed for so doing by the U.S. government on March 1. In short order he became a Confederate general, but died of poor health in 1862.)
[RR 1]

The time for compromise has now passed. The South is determined to maintain her position, and make all who oppose her smell Southern powder and feel Southern steel.
—Confederate President Jefferson Davis, speech, Montgomery, Alabama, February 16, 1861. (Davis was inaugurated as "provisional" president on February 18. His formal election came on November 6.)
[BCF]

We are without machinery, without means, and threatened by a powerful opposition; but I do not despond, and will not shrink from the task imposed upon me.
—Confederate President Jefferson Davis, February 20, 1861, in a letter to his wife. Davis was elected Confederate president on February 9.
[CW-1]

In *your* hands, my dissatisfied fellow countrymen, and not in *mine,* is the momentous issue of civil war. The government will not assail *you.* You can have no conflict without being yourselves the aggressors. *You* have no oath registered in heaven to destroy

❖❖❖

the government, while *I* shall have the most solemn one to "preserve, protect and defend" it.
——President Abraham Lincoln, first inaugural address, March 4, 1861
[GS]

One section of our country believes slavery is *right*, and ought to be extended, while the other believes it is *wrong*, and ought not to be extended. This is the only substantial dispute.
——President Abraham Lincoln, first inaugural address, March 4, 1861
[GS]

Our new government is founded upon . . . the great truth that the negro is not equal to the white man; that slavery . . . is his natural and normal condition. This, our new government, is the first in the history of the world based upon this great physical, philosophical, and moral truth. . . . The new Constitution has put to rest forever *all* the agitating questions relating to our peculiar institutions——African slavery as it exists among us——the proper *status* of the negro in our form of civilization.
——Confederate Vice President Alexander H. Stephens, speech in "vindication" of the Confederate Constitution, Savannah, Georgia, March 21, 1861
[RR 1]

✿

FORT SUMTER

Fort Sumter, South Carolina, was a symbol to the North and South before, during, and after the war. Situated on an island in the Charleston harbor, South Carolina felt the federal presence of the fort there an affront to the state's declared independence, and demanded the federal force's withdrawal. The fort's surrender on April 14, after two days of shelling, came to be seen as the war's beginning. The federal government had been attacked, thus justifying armed retaliation by the North. In 1864 Union forces destroyed Fort Sumter, and on April 14, 1865, after the

❖❖❖

surrender of the Confederacy's largest army, the Union once more established the Stars and Stripes above the site.

The firing on that fort will inaugurate a civil war greater than any the world has yet seen. . . .
      —Confederate Secretary of State Robert Toombs, April 1861
      [CW-1]

SIR: I have the honor to acknowledge the receipt of your communication, demanding the evacuation of this Fort, and to say in reply thereto that it is a demand with which I regret that my sense of honor and my obligations to my Government prevent my compliance.
      —Union Major Robert Anderson, commanding Fort Sumter, letter to Confederate General P. G. T. Beauregard, April 11, 1861
      [UR]

Gentlemen, if you do not batter us to pieces, we shall be starved out in a few days.
      —Union Major Robert Anderson, remark to Colonel James Chesnut, Captain Stephen D. Lee, and Lt. Colonel A. R. Chisholm, sent by Confederate General P. G. T. Beauregard with demands of surrender, April 11, 1861
      [CW-1]

MAJOR ANDERSON: By virtue of Brigadier General Beauregard's command, we have the honor to notify you that he will open the line of his batteries on Fort Sumter in one hour from this time.
      —Confederate General Pierre Gustave Beauregard's aide-de-camp's message to Union Major Robert Anderson, April 12, 1861
      [UR]

Our Southern brethren have done grievously wrong, they have rebelled and have attacked their father's house and their loyal brothers. They must be punished and brought back, but this necessity breaks my heart.
      —Union Major Robert Anderson, after surrendering Fort Sumter, April 14, 1861. The South had begun the war. (Anderson returned to Fort Sumter for its flag-raising four years later.)
      [WW]

———————❖❖❖———————

Fort Sumter is ours, and nobody is hurt. With mortar, Paixhan, and petard, we tender "Old Abe" our *Beau-regard.*

—Confederate President Jefferson Davis, quoted in the *Charleston Mercury,* April 16, 1861
[RR 1, Diary, 26]

Secession is our watchword; our rights we all demand;
And to defend our firesides we pledge our hearts and hand.
Jeff Davis is our President, with Stephens by his side;
Brave Beauregard, our General, will join us in the ride.

—"The Southern Wagon," anonymous
[CWT]

✿

After the attack on Fort Sumter, President Lincoln issued a call for 75,000 volunteers to prepare for the suppression of the rebellion. North and South began preparing for war, though neither side foresaw the war's length. Secession continued, with Virginia, Arkansas, North Carolina, and Tennessee withdrawing from the Union. Border state Missouri's loyalty was divided, claimed by the Union and the Confederacy. Kentucky, Maryland, and Delaware stayed in the Union, though the Confederacy made a long, strong stand in Kentucky. For the next few months, until late July, there was more talk than fighting while troops on both sides trained for battle. Many of the U.S. Army's most talented young officers "went South," to fight for the Confederacy.

Your dispatch is received. In answer, I say emphatically, Kentucky will furnish no troops for the wicked purpose of subduing her sister southern states.

—Kentucky Governor Beriah Magoffin, letter of April 16, 1861, in reply to Secretary of War Simon Cameron's call for troops. (Kentucky, birthplace of Abraham Lincoln and Jefferson Davis, stayed in the Union; on April 20, however, it announced it would stay "neutral" for the time being.)
[RR 1]

❖❖❖

Grant, O God, that all the efforts now being made to overthrow rebellion in our distracted country may be met with success. Let the forces that have risen against our Government, and Thy law, be scattered to the winds, and may no enemies be allowed to prevail against us. Grant, O God, that those who have aimed at the very heart of the republic may be overthrown. We ask Thee to bring those men to destruction, and wipe them from the face of the country!

 —Opening session prayer, New York East Methodist Conference, April 17, 1861

 [RR 1]

Well, my dearest one, Virginia has severed her connection with the Northern hive of abolitionists, and takes her stand as a sovereign and independent State.

 —John Tyler, in Richmond, Virginia, letter to his wife, April 17, 1861. Tyler, the former U.S. president and a Virginian, having failed to negotiate a compromise between the North and South, supported the Confederacy.

 [BG, 45]

You have made the greatest mistake of your life, but I feared it would be so.

 —Union General Winfield Scott, to Colonel Robert E. Lee, who declined Scott's offer to command the Union army, April 18, 1861

 [BCF]

With all my devotion to the Union, and the feeling of loyalty and duty of an American citizen, I have not been able to make up my mind to raise my hand against my relatives, my children, my home. I have, therefore, resigned my commission in the Army, and save in defense of my native State (with the sincere hope that my poor services may never be needed) I hope I may never be called upon to draw my sword.

 —Robert E. Lee, letter to his sister, April 20, 1861, from Arlington, Virginia. Lee wrote this three days after Virginia seceded and two days after he declined President Lincoln's and General Scott's offer of the command of the federal armies. (On April 22 Lee became the commander of the Military and Naval Forces of Virginia.)

 [CWT: ref: *Recollections and Letters of General Robert E. Lee*, 1904]

❖❖❖

I have served my country under the flag of the Union for more than fifty years, and as long as God permits me to live, I will defend that flag with my sword; even if my own native State assails it.

—Union General Winfield Scott, to "the Chairman of the committee appointed by the Virginia Convention to wait upon Gen. Scott and tender him the command of the forces of Virginia in this struggle," Washington, D.C., April 21, 1861
[RR 1, Doc, 78]

This war means one of two things—emancipation or disunion.

—Wendell Phillips, abolitionist, speech, Boston, April 21, 1861
[RR 1, Doc, 81]

Mind what I tell you: You fellows will catch the devil before you get through with this business.

—Union Admiral David Farragut, a native of Tennessee, to his fellow officers who quit the U.S. Navy and joined the Confederacy, 1861
[BCF]

Lincoln may bring his 75,000 troops against us. We fight for our homes, our fathers and mothers, our wives, brothers, sisters, sons, and daughters!

—Confederate Vice President Alexander H. Stephens, speech at Richmond, Virginia, April 22, 1861. (On April 15, President Lincoln had called for 75,000 volunteers to enlist for three months.)
[RR 1]

In independence we seek no conquest, no aggrandizement, no cession of any kind from the States with which we have lately confederated. All we ask is to be let alone.

—Confederate President Jefferson Davis, message to Congress, announcing the ratification of the Confederate Constitution, Montgomery, Alabama, April 29, 1861
[RR 1, Doc, 117]

❖❖❖

Any thing on earth and any form of government, any tyranny or despotism you will; but nothing on earth shall ever induce us to submit to any union with the brutal, bigoted blackguards of the New England States, who neither comprehend nor regard the feelings of gentlemen! Man, woman and child will die first!

—Citizen of Charleston, South Carolina, quoted by W. H. Russell, *London Times* reporter, April 30, 1861

[RR 1]

I long to be a man, but as I can't fight, I will content myself with working for those who can.

—Louisa May Alcott, author, diary, Concord, Massachusetts, April 1861. (In 1862 Alcott began working in a Washington, D.C., hospital.)

[WW]

. . . as a Christian I wouldn't like to see war, but as a soldier, sir, I would like to see war.

—Thomas J. "Stonewall" Jackson, a professor of Natural Philosophy at Virginia Military Institute, in Lexington, 1861. (His wife later denied he would ever say he desired war; in any case, Jackson brought his cadets to Richmond in April as drillmasters and organized his own brigade. Dubbed "Stonewall" at the First Battle of Bull Run, Jackson became one of the South's greatest generals.)

[CWT: ref: *The Long Arm of Lee*, 1915]

There are only two sides to the question. Every man must be for the United States or against it. There can no neutrals in this war; *only patriots—or traitors.*

—Stephen Douglas, speech on arrival at Chicago, to mayor and citizens, May 1, 1861. (Douglas died June 4.)

[RR 1, Doc, 204.5]

To our mind, there is but one easy, short and effectual way to suppress and put down the desolating war which the slaveholders and their rebel minions are now waging against the American Government and its loyal citizens. Fire must be met with water, darkness with light, and war for the destruction of liberty, must be met with war for the destruction of slavery. The

❖❖❖

simple way, then, to put an end to the savage and desolating war now waged by the slaveholders, is to strike down slavery itself, the primal cause of that war.

—Frederick Douglass, author and abolitionist, "How to End the War," in *Douglass' Monthly*, May 1861
[DM, 451]

I will receive 200 able-bodied men if they will present themselves at my headquarters by the first of June with good horse and gun. I wish none but those who desire to be actively engaged. My headquarters for the present is at Corinth, Miss. Come on, boys, if you want a heap of fun and to kill some Yankees.

—Confederate Lieutenant Colonel Nathan Bedford Forrest, recruitment notice, May 1861. (Forrest, a slave trader, became the South's most successful cavalry general, bedeviling the Union forces throughout the war.)
[CW-1; WW]

Nothing to do with Maynard rifle but load her up, turn her North, and pull trigger. If twenty of them don't clean out all Yankeedom, then I'm a liar, that's all.

—Confederate soldier from Mississippi, quoted in the *Oxford* [Mississippi] *Intelligencer,* 1861
[CWT]

I owe Virginia little, my country much. She has entrusted me with a distant command, and I shall remain under her flag as long as it waves the sign of the National Constitutional Government.

—Union Colonel P. St. George Cooke, Fort Crittenden, Utah, in response to Governor John Letcher of Virginia's call for "all natives of the State in the army and navy" to join it, June 6, 1861. (A naval lieutenant, W. K. Mayo, also replied negatively to the governor's call: "Though I am a Virginian by birth, I am no Southerner, nor Northerner, nor Western man. I am a citizen of the United States.")
[RR 2, 172]

❖❖❖

. . . O God I pray thee to Direct a bullet or a bayonet to pirce the Hart of every northern soldier that invades southern Soile and after the Body has Rendered up its Traterish Sole gave it a trators reward a Birth In the Lake of Fires and Brimstone my honest convicksion is that Every man wome and chile that has gave aide to the abolishionist are fit Subjects for Hell . . .

—Overseer, Magnolia Plantation, below New Orleans, diary, June 13, 1861
[JR]

Against the most beneficial Government, the most equal laws, and a system carrying within itself a recognized and peaceful mode of adjusting every real or imaginary wrong or hardship, a portion of the people of the United States—the least civilized, the least educated, the least industrious, without a single wrong specified on the part of the National Government—have risen in rebellion against it, robbing its treasuries, and even its hospitals; firing upon and treading under foot the flag of our country; menacing its Capital with armed hordes, led by the double-dyed traitors, who, educated at the cost of the nation, and sworn to defend its laws, have deserted in the hour of need and turned their arms against their nursing mother; and appealed to all the scoundrels of the world to come and take service under the Rebel flag, against the commerce of the United States.

—Charles King, president of Columbia College, New York City, address to the graduating class, June 26, 1861
[RR 2, p. 175]

The States have their *status* IN the Union, and they have no other *legal status*. If they break from this, they can only do so against law, and by revolution. The Union, and not themselves separately, procured their independence, and their liberty. By conquest, or purchase, the Union gave each of them whatever of independence, and liberty, it has.

—President Abraham Lincoln, message to Congress in special session, July 4, 1861
[GS]

❖❖❖

First Battle of Bull Run (Manassas)

On July 21, the first major battle of the war occurred about twenty-five miles south of Washington, D.C., near Manassas Junction, Virginia, and the stream called Bull Run, where two Confederate forces led by Generals P. G. T. Beauregard and Joseph Johnston encountered Union forces led by General Irwin McDowell. Washington, D.C., society traveled to the site to watch, as if it were a spectator sport. When the Confederates broke through the lines and began the rout, the spectators fled, blocking the roads for Union retreat. With this victory, the South was elated; the North was shocked.

If I could only get the enemy to attack me, as I am trying to have him do, I would stake my reputation on the handsomest victory that could be hoped for.

—Confederate General P. G. T. Beauregard, letter to Congressman L. T. Wigfall, July 8, 1861
[LL I, 42]

Sarah my love for you is deathless, it seems to bind me with mighty cables that nothing but Omnipotence could break; and yet my love of Country comes over me like a strong wind and bears me unresistibly on with all these chains to the battle field. . . . I have, I know, but few and small claims upon Divine Providence, but something whispers to me—perhaps it is the wafted prayer of my little Edgar, that I shall return to my loved ones unharmed. If I do not my dear Sarah, never forget how much I love you, and when my last breath escapes me on the battle field, it will whisper your name.

—Union soldier Sullivan Ballou, letter to his wife from Camp Clark, Washington, D.C., July 14, 1861. He died the next week at the First Battle of Bull Run.
[http://www.pbs.org/civilwar/war/ballou_letter.html]

Lord preserve the soul while I destroy the body.

—Confederate Colonel William N. Pendleton, chief of General Joseph Johnston's artillery and a minister, overheard at Manassas, as he fired at the Union army, July 21, 1861
[JR]

❖❖❖

I don't feel like dying yet.
—Confederate Major Roberdeau Wheat, when, shot through both lungs, he was told the wounds were fatal, First Battle of Bull Run, July 21, 1861. (According to D. S. Freeman, in *Lee's Lieutenants,* "The medical man held to his contention. 'There is no instance on record,' said he, 'of recovery from such a wound.' 'Well, then,' answered Wheat, in a phrase that became a lawyer, 'I will put my case upon record.'" Wheat did *not* die yet, and led his Louisiana Tigers until he was killed at the Battle of Gaines's Mill, Virginia, June 27, 1862.)
[LL, vol. 1, 88]

There is nothing like it this side of the infernal region, and the peculiar corkscrew sensation that it sends down your backbone under these circumstances can never be told. You have to *feel* it, and if you say you did not feel it, and heard the yell, then you have never *been* there.
—Union soldier describing the "rebel yell," a call that Stonewall Jackson thought "the sweetest music I ever heard." (Ambrose Bierce, a Union officer and author, after a later battle, remarked, "It was the ugliest sound that any mortal ever heard—even a mortal exhausted and unnerved by two days of hard fighting, without sleep, without rest, without food, and without hope.")
[CW-3; BCF]/[RR]

They have killed me, but never give up the field.
—Confederate Colonel Francis Bartow, dying words, at the First Battle of Bull Run, July 21, 1861
[CR]

With your first shot you become a new man. Personal safety is your least concern. Fear has no existence in your bosom. Hesitation gives way to an uncontrollable desire to rush into the thickest of the fight. The dead and dying around you, if they receive a passing thought, only serve to stimulate you to revenge.
—Confederate soldier, quoted in a Charleston newspaper, of his experiences at First Bull Run
[JR]

❖❖❖

There is Jackson standing like a stone wall! Let us determine to die here, and we will conquer.
> —Confederate General Barnard E. Bee, rallying his brigade near Henry House Hill, at the First Battle of Bull Run, July 21, 1861. (Bee thus coined Colonel Thomas J. Jackson's nickname, but was almost immediately wounded, and died the next day.)
> [CW-1/WW]

They may stay like that. I know I'm going home. I've had enough of fighting to last my lifetime.
> —Anonymous Union officer, entering Washington, D.C., after Bull Run, to the British journalist William Howard Russell, July 21, 1861 [BG, 111: ref: W. H. Russell, *My Diary North and South*, London: Bradbury & Evans, 1863]

Today will be known as BLACK MONDAY. We are utterly and disgracefully routed, beaten, whipped by secessionists.
> —George Templeton Strong, of New York City, diary, upon hearing of the Union loss at the First Battle of Bull Run, July 21, 1861 [GTS]

Whilst great credit is due to other parts of our gallant army, God made my brigade more instrumental than any other in repulsing the main attack. This is for your information only—say nothing about it. Let others speak praise, not myself.
> —Confederate Colonel Thomas "Stonewall" Jackson, letter to wife, from Manassas, July 22, 1861
> [TJJ]

I have left home and a good situation . . . and have grasped the weapon of death for the purpose of doing my part in defending and upholding the integrity, laws and the preservation of my adopted country from a band of contemptible traitors who would if they can accomplish their hellish designs, destroy the best and noblest government on earth, merely for the purpose of benefiting themselves on the slave question.
> —Union soldier Philip Smith, diary, July 22, 1861
> [BY]

❖❖❖

All this difficulty has been brought about by men who, because they could not rule, are determined to ruin.

—Ohio Senator John Sherman, in response to Kentucky Senator John Breckinridge, debate in the Senate, after Breckinridge objected to a Senate resolution by Andrew Johnson stating that the "present war was forced on the country by the disunionists in the South," July 25, 1861
[RR 2, 404]

I suggest to my reverend brethren of the clergy . . . that in the prayer for the President of the United States, etc., and in the prayer for Congress, also, the words "United States" be omitted, and the words "Confederate States" be substituted in their place.

—Bishop James Otey, letter to the clergy of the Protestant Episcopal Church in the diocese of Tennessee, July 31, 1861
[RR 2, 413]

✿

THE ASCENDANCY OF GEORGE B. MCCLELLAN

George B. McClellan, of Ohio, young (thirty-five when the war began), handsome, proud, was made Major General of the Department of Ohio on May 13, 1861. After winning a battle at Rich Mountain, Virginia, in July, he was chosen by General Winfield Scott to command the Division of the Potomac. When Scott retired on October 31, 1861, McClellan became commander in chief of the Union army.

No prospect of a brilliant victory shall induce me to depart from my intention of gaining success by maneuvering rather than by fighting. I will not throw these raw men of mine into the teeth of artillery and intrenchments if it is possible to avoid it.

—Union Major General George B. McClellan, July 12, 1861, Rich Mountain, western Virginia
[CW-1]

I find myself in a new and strange position here—President, cabinet, General Scott, and all deferring to me. By some strange

❖❖❖

operation of magic I seem to have become *the* power of the land. I almost think that were I to win some small success now I could become Dictator or anything else that might please me—but nothing of that kind would please me . . .

> —Union Major General George B. McClellan, letter to his wife, from Washington, D.C., July 27, 1861. (On this date President Lincoln named McClellan commander of the Division of the Potomac, replacing General Irvin McDowell.)
> [MOS, 82]

I shall carry this thing on "en grand" and crush the rebels in one campaign.

> —Union Major General George B. McClellan, letter to his wife, from Washington, D.C., August 2, 1861. (McClellan, whatever his talents, was full of bluster and never in a hurry.)
> [MOS, 83]

I have scarcely slept one moment for the last three nights, knowing well that the enemy intend some movement and fully recognizing our own weakness. If Beauregard does not attack tonight I shall look upon it as a dispensation of Providence—he *ought* to do it.

> —Union Major General George B. McClellan, letter to his wife, from Washington, D.C., August 8, 1861. (Nothing immediately came of this threat.)
> [MOS, 84]

We have had our last retreat. We have seen our last defeat. You stand by me, and I will stand by you, and henceforth victory will crown our efforts.

> —Union Major General George B. McClellan, address to the Pennsylvania regimental soldiers who were "anxious to wipe out Bull Run," September 10, 1861. (President Lincoln and his cabinet were in attendance.)
> [RR 3, Diary, 22]

The first thing in the morning is drill, then drill, then drill again. Then drill, drill, a little more drill. Then drill, and lastly drill.

❖❖❖

Between drills, we drill and sometimes stop to eat a little and have a roll-call.
>—Union soldier O. W. Norton, letter to a friend, from Camp Leslie, near Falls Church, Virginia, October 9, 1861
>[OWN, 28]

When I proposed that you should come here to aid, not supersede me, you had my friendship and confidence. You still have my confidence.
>—Union General in Chief Winfield Scott, to Major General George B. McClellan, at a War Department meeting, early October, 1861. (McClellan did supersede Scott in November.)
>[CW-1]

The army will unite with me in the feeling of regret that the weight of many years, and the effect of increasing infirmities, contracted and intensified in his country's service, should just now remove from our head the great soldier of our nation . . . a citizen who, in his declining years, has given to the world the most shining instancing of loyalty in disregarding all ties of birth, and clinging to the cause of truth and honor.
>—Union Major General George B. McClellan, General Order No. 19, on the resignation of Lieutenant General Winfield Scott as commander in chief, November 1, 1861
>[RR 3, 268]

I will hold McClellan's horse if he will only bring us success.
>—President Abraham Lincoln, remarking on Major General George B. McClellan's deliberate rudeness to him when Lincoln paid him a call, November 13, 1861
>[CW-1/BCF]

☼

DIVIDED MISSOURI AND THE WAR IN THE WEST

The border states included Missouri and Kentucky, with both states nominally remaining in the Union. In June, General Nathaniel Lyon led federal soldiers through Missouri and gained control of the Missouri River for the North. In July there

❖❖❖

*was a fight at Carthage, Missouri, where the Union was forced
to retreat by cavalry. On August 10, Missouri's largest battle of
the war took place at Wilson's Creek, near Springfield, where
the Confederates defeated the troops of General Lyon, who was
killed in the fight. The Union forces retreated to the southwest,
thus giving up much of the state to Confederate sympathizers.
Union Major General John C. Fremont, commander of the
Western Department, had a rift with President Lincoln when
Fremont issued an emancipation proclamation in Missouri that
declared free the slaves of any declared secessionists. Lincoln
was not ready to go this far yet, and ordered Fremont to rescind
the proclamation. Meanwhile, in September, Union Brigadier
General Ulysses S. Grant and his troops took Paducah,
Kentucky, at the mouth of the Tennessee River, helping to keep
the Confederates from dominating the state. In November,
Grant's forces raided Confederate-held Belmont, Missouri, and
then narrowly escaped capture.*

We were both missionaries and musketeers. When we captured
a man we talked him nearly to death; in other respects we
treated him humanely. The Civil War was a battle of ideas inter-
rupted by artillery.

—Union soldier, on the federal army's advance through divided
Missouri, June 1861
[CWDD, 86]

. . . leave your ploughs in the furrow, and your oxen in the yoke,
and rush like a tornado upon our invaders and foes, to sweep
them from the face of the earth, or force them from the soil of
our State! . . . We have plenty of ammunition, and the cattle on
ten thousand hills are ours.

—Confederate guerila M. Jeff Thompson, of the "Missouri State
Guard," proclamation to the people of Missouri, headquarters,
Missouri State Guards, Bloomfield, Missouri, August 1, 1861
[RR 2, Doc, 457]

❖❖❖

> Stand firmly by your cannon,
> Let ball and grape-shot fly,
> And trust in God and Davis,
> But keep your powder dry.

—Confederate verse, August 1861
[JR]

Be careful, Ulyss; you're a general now; it's a good job, don't lose it.

—Jesse Root Grant, Ulysses S. Grant's father, letter to his son, on U. S. Grant being made a brigadier general in the Western Army, August 8, 1861
[CW-1]

Real and personal property of those who shall take up arms against the United States, or who shall be directly proven to have taken an active part with their enemies in the field, is declared confiscated to public use, and their slaves, if any they have, are hereby declared free men.

—Union Major General John C. Fremont, proclamation from head-quarters, Western Department, St. Louis, Missouri, August 30, 1861. (On September 11, President Lincoln wrote Fremont, telling him that he could not supersede the August 6, 1861, act of Congress "on the same subject." Lincoln relieved Fremont of his duties on November 1, 1861.)
[RR 3, 33]

Whereas Major General John C. Fremont, commanding the minions of Abraham Lincoln, in the State of Missouri, has seen fit to declare martial law throughout the whole state, and has threatened to shoot any citizen soldier found in arms within certain limits; also to confiscate the property and free the negroes belonging to the members of the Missouri State Guards; therefore, know ye that I, M. Jeff Thompson, Brigadier General of the First Military District of Missouri . . . do most solemnly promise that, for every member of the Missouri State Guard or soldiers of our allies, the armies of the Confederate States, who shall be put to death in pursuance of the said order of General

❖❖❖

Fremont, I will *hang, draw,* and *quarter* a minion of said Abraham Lincoln.
—Confederate Brigadier General M. Jeff Thompson, headquarters, Missouri State Guards, Camp Hunter, September 2, 1861
[RR 3, 59]

Are we indeed slaves, that we are thus to be dragged in chains at the feet of despotic power? . . . Were our liberties given us but to be trampled beneath the feet of Abraham Lincoln?
—Confederate General Simon Bolivar Buckner, address to the "freemen of Kentucky," Russellville, Kentucky, September 12, 1861
[RR 3, 128]

Soldiers from Iowa, Nebraska, and Illinois—go home! We want you not here, and we thirst for your blood. We have not invaded your States, we have not polluted your hearth stones, therefore leave us; and after we have wiped out the Hessians and tories we will be your friendly neighbors if we cannot be your brothers.
—Confederate Brigadier General M. Jeff Thompson, proclamation from the headquarters of the First Military District of the Missouri State Guards, Camp in St. Francois County, October 14, 1861
[RR 3, Diary, 49]

We must have fifty thousand men. Give me these men, and, by the help of God, I will drive the hireling thieves and marauders from the State.
—Confederate Major General Sterling Price, proclamation issued at Neosho, Missouri, November 1861
[RR 3, Doc, 444]

At first some of the officers seemed to think that to be surrounded was to be placed in a hopeless position, where there was nothing to do but surrender. But when I announced that we had cut our way in and could cut our way out just as well, it seemed a new revelation to officers and soldiers.
—Brigadier General Ulysses S. Grant, reflecting on having taken a Confederate camp near Belmont, Missouri, which Confederate General Leonidas Polk then surrounded, November 7, 1861. (Grant and his troops did manage to "cut" their "way out.")
[USG]

❖❖❖

"Skirmish"! hell and damnation! I'd like to know what he calls a *battle*.
—Confederate General Leonidas Polk, after receiving a note from Union Brigadier General Ulysses S. Grant, mentioning their "skirmish" at Belmont, Missouri, November 7, 1861
[RR 3, Poetry, 71]

✿

North and South, there was suppression of unpopular or what were seen as treasonous views.

I am sorry that I have published what I have, and I promise that I will never again write or publish articles against the North and in favor of secession, so help me God.
—Ambrose L. Kimball, editor, *Essex County Democrat*, Haverhill, Massachusetts, on his knees to a mob after it tarred and feathered him and threatened him with further violence if he did not renounce his views, August 21, 1861. (On the same day, an item in the *Albany Journal* said: "Men and presses who are today preaching 'Compromise' and 'Peace,' are doing more to cripple the Government and help treason than the Rebel armies themselves.")
[RR 2, 71]

✿

THE SOUNDS OF WEAPONS

Throughout the war, soldiers and officers alike remarked on the sounds of the weaponry at the battles, and they tried, in letters and recollections, to reproduce such sounds on paper.

. . . the rifle and musket balls have been whizzing round our heads so much that we don't notice them as much as we would a bumble bee at home.
—Union Lieutenant Thomas McClure, diary, outside Lexington, Missouri, September 18, 1861
[RR 3, Doc, 81]

A Minie ball goes "Zip!" with the same sound as you make on a fiddle by giving the E string a pick and running your finger up on it; and the sound of a shell is as if it said: "WHERE ARE

YOU? *Where are you?* Where are you? Where are you?
FOUND YOU!" That last is when it bursts.
—Soldier Eli Billings
[CWT: ref: Clifton Johnson, *Highways and Byways from the St. Lawrence to Virginia,* 1913]

. . . the air seemed all alive with the sounds of various projectiles . . . from the spiteful, cat-like spit of the buckshot, the *pouf* of the old-fashioned musket ball and the *pee-ee-zing* of the minie bullet, to the roar of the ordinary shell and the *whoot-er whoot-er* of the Whitworth "mortar-pestle"; while the shrieks of wounded men and horses and the yells of the apparently victorious rebels added to the uproar.
—Anonymous Union soldier
[CW-3]

Bang, bang, bang, a rattle, de bang, bang, bang, a boom, de bang . . . whirr-siz-siz-siz—a ripping, roaring, boom, bang!
—Confederate soldier Sam Watkins
[SRW]

We were sometimes amused by the music of musket balls. One would come along with the *"meow"* of a kitten, and the men would declare the rebels were throwing kittens at them. Another would come with an angry howl, as if seeking its Yankee victim. And we listened to others that had the wailing sound of a winter's wind. All these sounds were more musical than the "zip" of the bullet at short range.
—Union soldier S. F. Fleharty
[BY]

So many men were daily struck in the camp and trenches that men became utterly reckless, passing about where balls were striking as though it was their normal life and making a joke of a narrow escape or a noisy, whistling ball.
—Union Major General David S. Stanley
[O.R. Series 1, Vol. 38, Pt. 1, 226]

❖❖❖

One of our men says he could hear it say, "secesh-secesh-seches, se-chong," as it landed in the water. Had one of these secesh villains hit us, it would have bored us through and through.

> —Union officer aboard the *Niagara,* on the Confederate shots from batteries at Forts McRea and Barrancas, Pensacola harbor, Florida, November 23, 1861
> [RR 3, 423]

You have no idea of the horrible noise the shells make—when one passes over your head with its scream as if fifty locomotive whistles were blowing at once, no man can help dodging.

> —Union surgeon Edwin Hutchinson, letter to his mother
> [BY]

✿

FALL 1861

The North began to see that it was going to take some time to win this war. There was division in the North between those eager for peace and those supporting the continuation of war to bring the seceded states back into the Union. Already the Confederacy and Union realized the cost of lives that resulted not from bullets and bombs, but from disease. Meanwhile, in the "Trent Affair," which almost precipitated a war with Great Britain, the Union ship San Jacinto *stopped a British mail ship, the* Trent, *and arrested two Confederate commissioners on board, John Slidell and James M. Mason, bound for England and France to try to enlist material and moral support for the South.*

The national edifice is on fire. Every man who can carry a bucket of water, or remove a brick, is wanted, but those who have the care of the building, having a profound respect for the feeling of the national burglars who set the building on fire, are determined that the flames shall only be extinguished by Indo-Caucasian hands, and to have the building burnt rather than

save it by means of any other. Such is the pride, the stupid prejudice and folly that rules the hour.

—Frederick Douglass, author and abolitionist, "Fighting Rebels
with Only One Hand," in his magazine, *Douglass' Monthly*,
September 1861. (It was not until 1862 that the Union allowed
African-Americans to serve as soldiers.)
[DM, 516]

I want to fight the rest of my life if necessary, before we recognize them as anything but Rebels and traitors who must be
humbled.

—Union soldier Charles Wills, letter to his sister, September 17,
1861
[WTFF]

Our poor sick, I know, suffer much. They bring it on themselves
by not doing what they are told. They are worse than children,
for the latter can be forced.

—Confederate General Robert E. Lee, letter to his wife, on the
lack of hygienic habits of the Southern volunteers, September 17,
1861. (Medical historians estimate 164,000 of the 750,000
Confederate soldiers died from disease and infections while about
80,000 were killed in fighting.)
[REL]

We operated in old blood-stained and often pus-stained coats,
the veterans of a hundred fights. We operated with clean hands
in the social sense, but they were undisinfected hands. . . . We
used undisinfected instruments from undisinfected plush-lined
cases, and still worse, used marine sponges which had been used
in prior pus cases and had been only washed in tap water. If a
sponge or an instrument fell on the floor it was washed and
squeezed in a basin of tap water and used as if it were clean.

—Union surgeon W. W. Keen, recollecting the medical workers'
lack of awareness of the benefits of hygiene
[DB, 124]

❖❖❖

I am very thankful to that God who withholds no good thing from me (though I am so utterly unworthy and ungrateful) for making me a Major General.

—Confederate Major General Stonewall Jackson, letter to his wife, October 7, 1861
[TJJ]

I exchange, with proud satisfaction, a term of six years in the United States Senate for the musket of a soldier.

—John C. Breckinridge, address to the people of Kentucky at Bowling Green, October 8, 1861. (Breckinridge, a former U.S. vice president, had lost to Lincoln in the race for president in 1860. He became a Confederate major general, and at the close of the war the Confederacy's secretary of war.)
[RR 3, Diary, 62]

Appealing to that sacred right of protest and resistance which is inherent in all oppressed communities and with a firm trust in the Almighty Ruler of Mankind, whose good providence is declared in history, and who can never tolerate the permanent ascendancy of wrong, we do hereby, on behalf of the people of North Carolina, deliberately and solemnly proclaim our independence of the spurious Government designating itself the Confederate States of America, and the revolutionary and treasonable dynasty which now usurps the governing power of our own State. We repudiate the unwarranted abrogations of authority asserted by these bold, bad men—traitors alike to the Federal Union and to the people of North Carolina.

—Marble Nash Taylor, Caleb B. Stowe, William O'Neil, resolutions adopted by the convention in Hyde County, statement of grievances, Hatteras, Hyde County, North Carolina, October 15, 1861. These men were citizens who protested North Carolina's secession "against the express wishes of a majority of 35,000 of her citizens" when the North Carolina assembly "refused to submit the obnoxious [secession] document to the people."
[RR 3, Doc, 178]

❖❖❖

I shall go to jail, as John Rogers went to the stake—for my *principles*. I shall go, because I have failed to recognize the hand of God in the work of breaking up the American Government, and the inauguration of the most wicked, cruel, unnatural, and uncalled-for war ever recorded in history. I go, because I have refused to laud to the skies the acts of tyranny, usurpation, and oppression, inflicted upon the people of East Tennessee, because of their devotion to the Constitution and laws of the Government, handed down to them by their fathers, and the liberties secured to them by a war of seven long years of gloom, poverty, and trial!

—Parson William G. Brownlow, editor of the *Knoxville Whig*, announcing the shutdown of his newspaper due to his arrest and pending trial by the "Confederate authorities," October 26, 1861. (In 1865, Brownlow was elected governor of Tennessee.)
[RR 3, Doc, 243]

Citizens of South Carolina: The civilized world stands appalled at the course you are pursuing!—Appalled at the crime you are committing against your own mother; the best, the most enlightened, and heretofore the most prosperous of nations. You are in a state of active rebellion against the laws of your country.

—Union General William Tecumseh Sherman, proclamation, after taking Port Royal, South Carolina, November 8, 1861. (The next day, Sherman, suffering from "nervous strain," was replaced by General Don Carlos Buell.)
[RR 3,11]

I yield to force under protest.

—Confederate diplomat James Mason, on his arrest by the United States while aboard the British *Trent*, bound for England, November 8, 1861. (His and his fellow diplomat Slidell's arrest set off a controversy in England, and threatened British-American relations. The U.S. held Mason and Slidell until December 26.)
[RR 3, 326]

❖❖❖

Whereas Negro Slavery is the origin and foundation of our National troubles, and the cause of the terrible rebellion in our midst, that is seeking to overthrow our Government; and whereas Slavery is incompatible with the Word of God, detrimental to the interests of a free people, as well as wrong to the slaves themselves; therefore, *Resolved,* that this Convention inquire into the expediency of making the proposed new State a free State, and that a provision be inserted in the Constitution for the gradual emancipation of all slaves within the proposed boundaries of the new State, to be submitted to the people of the same, for their approval or rejection.

—Mr. Hagan, of Boone County, resolution offered at the convention of Western Virginia, Wheeling, Virginia, December 8, 1861. (West Virginia became a state on June 20, 1863.)
[RR 3, Diary, 100]

❖❖❖

1862

The winter of 1861–1862 was particularly cold; the soldiers on both sides, camping far from home, suffered while awaiting the coming battles. As 1862 proceeded, the North began clipping off pieces of the Confederacy and rejoining them to the Union, while the South hunkered down with the realization that win or lose it would suffer deprivation due to the North's blockade of its ports. The Union army's commander in chief, George B. McClellan, was quite ill this winter, and President Lincoln worried that the Army of the Potomac would remain idle. Lincoln was also concerned that Major General Henry Halleck and Don Carlos Buell were failing to coordinate their efforts in the West. By the fall of this year Lincoln would acknowledge that the war's purpose was not only union but also emancipation and the eradication of slavery.

When I say that this rebellion has its source and life in slavery, I only repeat a simple truism.
  —U.S. Congressman George W. Julian, House speech, January 14, 1862
  [BCF]

To let this occasion pass unimproved, for getting rid of slavery, would be a sin against unborn generations.
  —Frederick Douglass, author and abolitionist, speech, Philadelphia, January 14, 1862
  [WW]

The country must now be roused to make the greatest effort that it will be called upon to make during the war. No matter

what the sacrifice may be, it must be made, and without loss of time. . . . All the resources of the Confederacy are now needed for the defense of Tennessee.
   —Confederate General Albert Sidney Johnston, January 22, 1862
   [CW-1]

The Southern people are not sufficiently alive to the necessity of exertion in the struggle they are involved in. Better to fight even at the risk of losing battles, than remain inactive to fill up inglorious graves.
   —*Richmond Examiner,* editorial, February 4, 1862
   [CWDD, 166]

In the beauty of the lilies Christ was born across the sea,
With a glory in his bosom that transfigures you and me:
As He died to make men holy, let us die to make men free,
While God is marching on.
   —Julia Ward Howe's "Battle Hymn of the Republic," published in *The Atlantic* in February 1862, was soon set to music.
   [CWP]

&

FORTS HENRY AND DONELSON CAMPAIGN

The Union's capture of Fort Henry, February 6, and Fort Donelson, February 16, in Tennessee was important in cracking through the Southern line, as the Tennessee and Cumberland rivers and thus most of Kentucky came under Northern control. Tennessee was now vulnerable to further inroads by the Union armies. Fort Donelson also brought Brigadier General Ulysses S. Grant to the notice of the eager and appreciative North. (His first two initials, it became said, stood for "Unconditional Surrender," for the terms by which Grant asked General Buckner to give up the fort.)

You have been wanting a fight; you have got it. Hell's before you!
   —Union General Lewis Wallace, to his men, preparatory to the attack on Fort Donelson, Tennessee, February 14, 1862
   [CW-1]

❖❖❖

Some of our men are pretty badly demoralized, but the enemy must be more so, for he has attempted to force his way out, but has fallen back: the one who attacks first now will be victorious and the enemy will have to be in a hurry if he gets ahead of me.
—Union Brigadier General Ulysses S. Grant, to his officers, at Fort Donelson, after a day of heavy casualties, February 15, 1862
[USG]

Gentlemen, troops do not have six days' rations served out to them in a fort if they mean to stay there. These men mean to retreat—not to fight. We will attack at once.
—Union Brigadier General Ulysses S. Grant, to his officers, after interrogating a Confederate deserter, February 15, 1862, the night before the attack on Fort Donelson
[RR 1]

No terms except an unconditional and immediate surrender can be accepted. I propose to move immediately upon your works.
—Union Brigadier General Ulysses S. Grant, note of reply to Confederate General Simon B. Buckner, who was holding Fort Donelson, Tennessee, February 16, 1862. (In his *Memoirs,* Grant recalled of the surrender: "I had been at West Point three years with Buckner and afterwards served with him in the army, so that we were quite well acquainted. In the course of our conversation, which was very friendly, he said to me that if he had been in command I would not have got up to Donelson as easily as I did. I told him that if he had been in command I should not have tried in the way I did. . . . ")
[USG]

Boys, these people are talking about surrendering, and I am going out of this place before they do or bust hell wide open.
—Confederate Lieutenant Colonel Nathan Bedford Forrest, to his cavalry, at Fort Donelson, February 16, 1862. (Before dawn on this morning, the day Fort Donelson was surrendered to General Grant, Forrest went to a council of Generals Floyd, Buckner, and Pillow, and told them, "I have a fine regiment of cavalry here, and I want permission to take it out. Grant me this much, and I'm off." Granted permission, Forrest and his cavalry of seven hundred escaped across a wintry stream.)
[RR 8, Poetry, 37]

❖❖❖

It is much less a job to take them than to keep them.

–Union Brigadier General Ulysses S. Grant, on the capture of Confederates after taking Fort Donelson, February 16, 1862. (Grant paroled or allowed to escape many of the prisoners.) General Buckner surrendered more than 12,000 men, and this capture led to President Lincoln's naming Grant a major general on February 17.

[CW-1]

We can whip you even-handed on land, but damn your gunboats!

—Confederate prisoner of war, taken at Fort Donelson, to a Northern newspaper correspondent

[RR 4, Doc, 211]

If I had captured him, I would have turned him loose, I would rather have him in command of you fellows than as a prisoner.

—Union Brigadier General Ulysses S. Grant speaking to Confederate General Simon B. Buckner, about Confederate General Gideon Pillow, who had fled Fort Donelson, Tennessee, before Grant's force captured it, February 16, 1862. (Grant later wrote in his *Memoirs,* "I had known General Pillow in Mexico, and judged that with any force, no matter how small, I could march up to within gunshot of any intrenchments he was given to hold.")

[CW-1]

If there is a man in all the country that does not rejoice over the news of today, frown on him, brand him as a traitor. Is he in your churches? Turn him out. Is he in your assembly? Put him out. Is he in your family? Shut the door in his face. We want it understood as the voice of the meeting, that the government is to hang all guilty traitors; and that if England continues to threaten, we will next pay our respects to her.

—Ohio Governor David Tod, to his legislature, State House, Columbus, Ohio, having called a meeting "to rejoice over the recent victories of Forts Henry and Donelson," February 17, 1862

[RR 4, Diary, 34]

❖❖❖

Even with the disappointment of the loss of Forts Henry and Donelson, Jefferson Davis, as well as the Confederacy's other leaders, urged the South to continue its hard fight.

My hope is reverently fixed on Him whose favor is ever vouchsafed to the cause which is just.

—Confederate President Jefferson Davis, second oath as president, Richmond, Virginia, February 22, 1862. (After serving one year as provisional president, Davis, elected without opposition in November, was inaugurated a second time as president for a six-year term.)
[CW-1]

The foot of the oppressor is on the soil of Georgia. He comes with lust in his eye, poverty in his purse, and hell in his heart. He comes a robber and a murderer. How shall you meet him? With the sword at the threshold! With death for him or for yourself! But more than this—let every woman have a torch, every child a firebrand—let the loved home of youth be made ashes, and the fields of our heritage be made desolate. Let blackness and ruin mark your departing steps if depart you must, and let a desert more terrible than Sahara welcome the vandals. Let every city be levelled by the flames, and every village be lost to ashes.

—Georgia legislators Howell Cobb, R. Toombs, M. J. Crawford, Thomas R. R. Cobb, address to the people of Georgia, February 1862
[RR 4, Doc, 192]

✿

THE *MERRIMACK* AND *MONITOR*

The Merrimack *was a Union ship salvaged and rebuilt by the Confederacy as the war's and the world's first ironclad fighting ship. Renamed the* Virginia, *it wreaked havoc on the Union navy and caused some panic in the North until the Union's own ironclad, the* Monitor, *faced off with it in the waters of Hampton Roads, Virginia.*

❖❖❖

Never before was anything like it dreamed of by the greatest enthusiast in maritime warfare.

> —Union Captain G. J. Van Brunt of the *Minnesota,* report after the fight in which the *Minnesota's* shots and shells bounced off the *Virginia (Merrimack),* March 8, 1862
> [RR 4, Doc, 267]

Not unlikely, we shall have a shell or a cannonball from one of her guns in the White House before we leave this room.

> —Secretary of War Edwin Stanton, on the Confederates' ironclad ram *Virginia,* March 8, 1862. (The *Virginia* had sunk or destroyed several Union ships at Hampton Roads, Virginia, and seemed indestructible. The next day the *Virginia* faced off with the Union *Monitor.*)
> [CW-1]

I experienced a peculiar sensation; I do not think it was fear, but it was different from anything I ever knew before. We were enclosed in what we supposed to be an impenetrable armor— we knew that a powerful foe was about to meet us—ours was an untried experiment and our enemy's fire might make a coffin for us all.

> —Union Lieutenant William F. Keeler, aboard the ironclad *Monitor,* Hampton Roads, Virginia, March 9, 1862
> [WW]

We thought at first it was a raft on which one of the *Minnesota's* boilers was being taken to shore for repairs.

> —Confederate sailor aboard the *Virginia,* on his first sight of the U.S.S. *Monitor,* the morning of March 9, 1862
> [BCF]

I guess she took us for some kind of a water tank. You can see surprise in a ship just as you can see it in a man, and there was surprise all over the *Merrimack.*

> —*Monitor* crewman, aboard the ironclad *Monitor,* Hampton Roads, Virginia, March 9, 1862. (The ironclad *Monitor,* designed by John Ericsson, met and battled for two hours to a draw the Confederate ironclad ram *Virginia.* About two months later, after

❖❖❖

McClellan's army advanced over the Virginia Peninsula, and took the town of Norfolk, the ironclad's port, the *Virginia* was scuttled by evacuating Confederate soldiers on May 11, 1862.)
[CW-1]

✿

At about the same time as the Monitor *and* Merrimack *fight, the largest battle of the war in the West occurred at Pea Ridge, Arkansas, by which the Confederacy effectively lost its hold in Missouri. The South was also dealing with shortages and changes in domestic life.*

The enemy is again far away in the Boston Mountains. The scene is silent and sad—the vulture and the wolf now have the dominion and the dead friends and foes sleep in the same lonely graves.
    —Union General Samuel Curtis, Commander of the Army of the Southwest, after three days of battle that ousted the Confederate forces from Pea Ridge (or Elkhorn Tavern), Arkansas, letter to his brother, March 8
[CWDD, 180]

> My homespun dress is plain, I know,
> My hat's palmetto, too;
> But then it shows what Southern girls
> For Southern rights will do.
> We have sent the bravest of our land
> To battle with the foe
> And we will lend a helping hand—
> We love the South you know.

    —"The Homespun Dress," anonymous
[TT]

We want cannon as greatly as any people who ever, as history tells you, melted their church-bells to supply them; and I, your general, entrusted with the command of the army embodied of your sons, your kinsmen and your neighbors, do now call on you to send your plantation-bells to the nearest railroad depot, subject to my order, to be melted into cannon for the defence of your plantations.

—Confederate General P. G. T. Beauregard, order to the planters of the Mississippi Valley, from headquarters of the Army of the Mississippi, Jackson, Tennessee, March 8, 1862
[RR 4, Doc, 294]

The rebels can afford to give up all their church bells, cow bells and dinner bells to Beauregard, for they never go to church now, their cows have all been taken by foraging parties, and they have no dinner to be summoned to.

—Louisville *Courier,* March 1862
[CW-1]

Far better would it be for the Atlantic Ocean with one swell surge to rise up and sweep us and all we have into the Pacific than for the infernal hell-hounds who wage this wicked war on us to triumph. Let any cruelties, any torments, any death that earth can inflict, come upon us in preference to the triumph of the Yankees!

—*Atlanta Confederacy,* editorial, March 20, 1862
[RR 4, Poetry, 100]

It seemed like tearing out my heart to give up the old Union, but when Alabama voted to separate, I thought it my duty to sustain her.

—A planter of Madison County, Alabama, after the Union forces took Huntsville, April 11, 1862. (The planter now swore to return to his old "allegiance.")
[RR 4, Doc, 469]

✿

SHILOH

The famous and bloody battle of Shiloh, or Pittsburg Landing, Tennessee, April 6–7, caught General Grant's Union forces by surprise, and they lost the first day's battle, but recovered by the second day to force a Confederate retreat. Both sides claimed

❖❖❖

victory, and Grant was blamed by some in the North for the
numerous casualties his men suffered. Shiloh came to be seen,
however, as an important Union victory, as the Confederacy
were forced to pull out of large areas of Tennessee.

Instead of relieving you, I wish you, as soon as your new army is
in the field, to assume immediate command, and lead it to new
victories.
   —Union Commander of Missouri Major General Henry Halleck,
   letter to General Ulysses S. Grant, Pittsburg Landing (Shiloh),
   Tennessee, March 17, 1862. ("Thus in less than two weeks after the
   victory at Donelson, the two leading generals in the army [Halleck
   and McClellan] were in correspondence as to what disposition
   should be made of me, and in less than three weeks I was virtually
   in arrest and without a command." Halleck's specific complaint was
   that Grant had not kept in contact with the commander, but there
   were rumors as well that Grant had drinking problems. Then,
   Halleck surprised him with this appointment as second in command
   of the Western armies.)
   [USG]

I have put you in motion to offer battle to the invaders of your
country. With the resolution and disciplined valor becoming
men fighting, as you are, for all worth living or dying for, you can
but march to a decisive victory over the agrarian mercenaries
sent to subjugate and despoil you of your liberties, property, and
honor. Remember the precious stake involved; remember the
dependence of your mothers, your wives, your sisters, and your
children on the result; remember the fair, broad, abounding
land, the happy homes, and the ties that would be desolated by
your defeat.
   —Confederate General Albert Sidney Johnston, notice to the Army
   of the Mississippi, Corinth, Mississippi, April 3, 1862
   [O.R. Series 1, Vol. 10, Part 2, 389]

I have no doubt that nothing will occur to-day more than some
picket firing. The enemy is saucy, but got the worst of it yesterday, and will not press our pickets far. I will not be drawn out far

unless with certainty of advantage, and I do not apprehend anything like an attack on our position.

—Union Brigadier General William Tecumseh Sherman, who dismissed reports of a Confederate buildup opposite his position at Pittsburg Landing (Shiloh), Tennessee, to Major General Ulysses S. Grant, April 5, 1862
[O.R. Series 1, Vol. 10, Pt. 2, p. 94]

My God, we're attacked!

—Union Brigadier General William Tecumseh Sherman, encountering the shots that killed his orderly, Thomas Holliday, at Shiloh, the morning of April 5, 1862. (From here on, Sherman rallied his men.)
[BCF]

The gory corpses lying all about us, in every imaginable attitude, and slain by an inconceivable variety of wounds, were shocking to behold.

—Union soldier, recalling the first day's battle at Shiloh, April 5, 1862
[BCF]

I would fight them if they were a million. They can present no greater front between those two creeks than we can, and the more men they crowd in there, the worse we can make it for them.

—Confederate General Albert Sidney Johnston, to his officers, at Shiloh, Tennessee, April 6, 1862. (Johnston was shot and killed the same day.)
[CW-1]

We this morning attacked the enemy in strong position in front of Pittsburg, and after a severe battle of ten hours, thanks be to the Almighty, gained a complete victory, driving the enemy from every position. Loss on both sides heavy, including our commander-in-chief, General A. S. Johnston, who fell gallantly leading his troops into the thickest of the fight.

—Confederate General P. G. T. Beauregard, report to Richmond, after the first day's battle at Shiloh, Tennessee, April 6, 1862
[O.R. Series 1, Vol. 10, Pt. 1, 384]

❖❖❖

The attack on my forces has been very spirited from early this morning. The appearance of fresh troops in the field now would have a disheartening effect, both by inspiring our men and disheartening the enemy.

> —Union Major General Ulysses S. Grant, letter to the commanding officer of the Advance Forces, April 6, 1862
> [O.R. Series 1, Vol. 10, Pt. 2, 95]

Retreat? No. I propose to attack at daylight and whip them.

> —Union Major General Ulysses S. Grant, to his generals, after the first day's battle at Shiloh, April 6, 1862, when his troops seemed overwhelmed.
> [WW]

We can hold them off till tomorrow; then they'll be exhausted, and we'll go at them with fresh troops.

> —Union Major General Ulysses S. Grant, in conversation, after the first day's battle at Shiloh, April 6, 1862
> [RR 4, 393]

Do you not think our troops are very much in the condition of a lump of sugar thoroughly soaked with water, but yet preserving its original shape, though ready to dissolve? Would it not be judicious to get away with what we have?

> —Confederate officer, to General P. G. T. Beauregard, during the second afternoon's fighting at Shiloh, Tennessee, April 6, 1862
> [BCF]

Ifs defeated the Confederates at Shiloh. There is little doubt that we would have been disgracefully beaten *if* all the shells and bullets fired by us had passed harmlessly over the enemy and *if* all of theirs had taken effect.

> —Union Major General Ulysses S. Grant, sarcastically reflecting in his *Memoirs* on how the death of Confederate General Albert Sidney Johnston effected the outcome at Shiloh, April 6, 1862
> [USG]

❖❖❖

You have slain all my men and cattle, and you may take the battery and be damned.
—A Confederate artillery chief, to a Union private, W. W. Worthington, at Shiloh, Tennessee, April 7, 1862
[UR]

Gentle winds of Springtime seem a sighing over a thousand new made graves.
—Union soldier, letter after Shiloh, April 7, 1862
[CWDD, 196]

Shiloh was the severest battle fought at the West during the war, and but few in the East equalled it for hard, determined fighting. I saw an open field, in our possession on the second day, over which the Confederates had made repeated charges the day before, so covered with dead that it would have been possible to walk across the clearing, in any direction, stepping on dead bodies, without a foot touching the ground.
—Union Major General Ulysses S. Grant, reflecting on the victory at Shiloh
[USG]

I did not think any more of seeing a man shot down by my side than you would of seeing a dumb beast killed. Strange as it may seem to you, but the more men I saw killed the more reckless I became.
—Union soldier Franklin Bailey, letter to his parents, after the battle at Shiloh, April 8, 1862
[BY]

The scenes on this field would have cured anybody of war. Mangled bodies, dead, dying in every conceivable shape, without heads, legs; and horses!
—Union General William Tecumseh Sherman, letter to his wife, from Camp Shiloh, April 11, 1862
[HLGS, 222–223]

On Shiloh's dark and bloody ground, the dead and wounded lay.
Amongst them was a drummer boy, that beat the drum that day.
A wounded soldier raised him up, His drum was by his side.

———— ❖❖❖ ————

He clasped his hands and raised his eyes and prayed before
  he died:
Look down upon the battle field, Oh Thou, our Heav'nly
  friend,
Have mercy on our sinful souls. The soldiers cried, "Amen."
For gather'd round a little group, Each brave man knelt and
  cried.
They listen'd to the drummer boy who prayed before he died.
  —"The Drummer Boy of Shiloh," song by William Shakespeare
  Hay, of Louisville
  [CR]

I can't spare this man. He fights.
  —President Abraham Lincoln, after Shiloh, resisting the call for
  General Ulysses S. Grant to be dismissed. General Halleck had
  taken over the field command from Grant.
  [AC]

What I want, and what the people want, is generals who will
fight battles and win victories. Grant has done this, and I propose to stand by him.
  —President Abraham Lincoln to General John Thayer, in the midst
  of the outcry against Grant
  [LAL]

❖

PENINSULAR CAMPAIGN AND THE SEVEN DAYS' BATTLES

*President Lincoln and General George B. McClellan disagreed
about strategy, but more importantly, Lincoln was frustrated
with McClellan's pace. McClellan frequently overestimated his
opponents' numbers, and made deliberation and caution his
most distinctive characteristics. Lincoln thought McClellan's
troops could advance overland from the north directly at the
Confederate army defending Richmond while McClellan
insisted on a "Peninsular campaign," whereby his troops, carried down the coast in ships, would land far down the Virginia
Peninsula, southeast of the Confederate capital, then advance.
McClellan began moving his troops by water in March, and in*

❖❖❖

early April the advance by land began. McClellan's giant force never reached Richmond, but he did bring his army as far as Harrison's Landing before having to abandon his plan for taking Petersburg. With the main body of the army no longer between the Confederacy and the capital, Lincoln often worried that Washington, D.C., was inadequately defended. After Confederate General Joseph Johnston was wounded at the Battle of Seven Pines on May 31, General Robert E. Lee took command of an army that he would make famous as the Army of Northern Virginia.

This section extends over several months, from February into July, during one of the most active periods of the war. The reader will then march again through the spring of 1862 and into summer with other campaigns and incidents.

Does not your plan involve a larger expenditure of *time* and *money* than mine? Wherein is a victory more certain by your plan than mine? Wherein is a victory *more valuable* by your plan than mine? In fact, would it not be *less* valuable in this, that it would break no great line of the enemy's communication, while mine would? In case of disaster, would it not be more difficult to retreat by your plan than mine?

　—President Abraham Lincoln, letter to Major General George B. McClellan, objecting to McClellan's plan to attack up the Virginia Peninsula rather than invade down through Virginia, February 3, 1862
　[UR, 96]

I am to watch over you as a parent over his children; and you know that your general loves you from the depths of his heart. It shall be my care, as it ever has been, to gain success with the least possible loss; but I know that, if necessary, you will willingly follow me to our graves for our righteous cause.

　—Union Major General George B. McClellan, at the graduation exercise of his army, Fairfax Court House, Virginia, March 1862
　[CW-1]

❖❖❖

Soldiers of the Army of the Potomac! For a long time I have
kept you inactive, but not without a purpose; you were to be disciplined, armed and instructed; the formidable artillery you now
have, had to be created; other armies were to move and accomplish certain results. I have held you back that you might give
the death-blow to the rebellion that has distracted our once
happy country. The patience you have shown, and your confidence in your General, are worth a dozen victories.
> —Union Major General George B. McClellan, address to the Army
> of the Potomac, from headquarters, Fairfax Court House, Virginia,
> March 14, 1862
> [RR 4, Doc, 306]

> What are you waiting for, George, I pray?—
> To scour your cross-belts with fresh pipe-clay?
> To burnish your buttons, to brighten your guns;
> Or wait you for May-day and warm Spring suns?
> Are you blowing your fingers because they are cold,
> Or catching your breath ere you take a hold?
> Is the mud knee-deep in valley and gorge?
> What are you waiting for, tardy George?

> —"Tardy George," song by George H. Boker, about Union Major
> General George B. McClellan's reluctance to engage in battle,
> winter 1862
> [UR, 97]

The President very coolly telegraphed me yesterday that he
thought I had better break the enemy's lines at once. I was
tempted to reply that he had better come and do it himself.
> —Union Commander in Chief Major General George B.
> McClellan, letter to his wife, April 8, 1862
> [MOS, 308]

Once more let me tell you that it is indispensable to *you* that you
strike a blow. I am powerless to help this. . . . The country will not
fail to note—is now noting—that the present hesitation to move
upon an intrenched enemy is but the story of Manassas repeated.
> —President Abraham Lincoln, letter to Commander in Chief Major
> General George B. McClellan, whose force was almost immediately
> delayed on the Peninsular Campaign, April 9, 1862
> [CW-1]

❖❖❖

No one but McClellan could have hesitated to attack.

—Confederate General Joseph Johnston, letter to General Robert
E. Lee, after Union Major General George B. McClellan failed to
move on the weak defenses of Yorktown, Virginia, April 22, 1862
[BCF]

Why, sir, it was just like sap-boiling in that stream—the bullets
fell so thick.

—Union soldier Julian A. Scott, fifteen years old, from Lamoille
County, Vermont, describing his company being shot at as they
crossed a stream, near Lee's Mill, Virginia, April 16, 1862
[RR 4, Doc, 503]

So now I am minus a leg! But never mind, dear parents. I suffer
but little pain, and will [be] home in a few weeks, I think.

—Union soldier William V. H. Cortelyou, Company B, 9th
Regiment, New York Volunteers, letter home from U.S. General
Hospital, Fortress Monroe, Virginia, April 26, 1862. (Cortelyou had
been wounded that week at South Mills, Virginia.)
[RR 4, Doc, 479]

The Fortieth Alabama regiment have been sitting very quiet for
the last four hours, listening to our guns belching vengeance to
your lines. You might as well attempt to change the run of the
James River as to subjugate the Confederacy.

—Confederate Company K, 40th Alabama, note to "General
McClellan and Command," Yorktown, May 2, 1862
[RR 5, 11]

I think the time is near when you must either attack Richmond
or give up the job and come to the defense of Washington.

—President Abraham Lincoln, message to Major General George
B. McClellan, May 25, 1862
[CWDD, 216]

Arragh, go in, b'ys! Bate the bloody spalpeens and revinge me
husband and God be wid yez!

—Union nurse Bridget Divers, who was tending to her husband's
wounds at Fair Oaks, Virginia, May 31, 1862. Her words were cred-
ited with inspiring the soldiers to charge.
[CWD]

———————— ❖❖❖ ————————

Charge 'em like hell, boys; show 'em you *are* damned Yankees.
—Union Colonel E. E. Cross, Fifth New Hampshire, leading his
men at the Battle of Fair Oaks, May 31 or June 1, 1862. (The
Confederates then wounded Cross in his head and leg.)
[RR 5, 93]

Good leg, thou wast a faithful friend,/ And truly hast thy duty
done;/ I thank thee most that to the end/ Thou didst not let this
body run./ Strange paradox! that in the fight/ Where I of thee
was thus bereft,/ I lost my left leg for "the Right,"/ And yet the
right's the one that's left!/ But while the sturdy stump remains,/
I may be able yet to patch it,/ For even now I've taken pains/ To
make an L-E-G to match it.
—"L-E-G on My Leg," by "a soldier in the hospital at New Haven,
who lost his leg in the battle of Fair Oaks," June 1, 1862
[RR 6, Poetry, 12]

> Oh the weather is bad and the whisky bad,
> Bad luck to the mud and the drizzle,
> Though they chop us up like sausage meat,
> The war is a murthering fizzle.
> The Rebs have taken the best of me legs,
> Bad luck to the chap that hit it,
> If Uncle Sam gives me a cork for me stump,
> I hope 'twill be one that will fit it.

—Song by Union amputees, who often made jokes about their
plight
[DB, 163]

Soldiers! I will be with you in this battle, and share its dangers
with you. Our confidence in each other is now founded upon
the past. Let us strike the blow which is to restore peace and
union to this distracted land.
—Union Major General George B. McClellan, address to the soldiers of the Army of the Potomac, from his headquarters, near New
Bridge, Virginia, June 3, 1862
[RR 5, 88]

❖❖❖

It is hard to see incompetence losing opportunity and wasting hard-gotten means, but harder still to bear is the knowledge that there is no available remedy.

—Confederate President Jefferson Davis, letter to his wife, June 3, 1862. (Downhearted in spite of the Confederate armies' fine showing this spring, Davis rarely confessed his anxiety to the public, confiding his worries instead in his wife and Robert E. Lee.)
[CWDD, 22]

Our people are opposed to work. Our troops, officers, community and press all ridicule and resist it. It is the very means by which McClellan has and is advancing. Why should we leave to him the whole advantage of labor. Combined with valour, fortitude and boldness, of which we have our fair proportion, it should lead us to success. What carried the Roman soldiers into all countries, but this happy combination? There is nothing so military as labor, and nothing so important to an army as to save the lives of its soldiers.

—Confederate General Robert E. Lee, letter to President Jefferson Davis, from headquarters near Richmond, June 5, 1862
[REL]

"Thank God," said a man with his leg amputated, "that it was not my right arm, for then I could never have fought again; as soon as this stump is well I shall join Stuart's cavalry; I can ride with a wooden leg as well as a real one."

—Judith McGuire, diary, Richmond, Virginia, June 9, 1862
[TT]

Gentlemen, in ten minutes every man must be in his saddle!

—Confederate General J. E. B. Stuart, to his cavalry, before they set off on a four-day ride around McClellan's Army of the Potomac, on the Virginia Peninsula, June 12, 1862. (This was a scouting mission that attracted Stuart by its risk and daring, and it gained him and his cavalry great fame.)
[CWDD, 225]

❖❖❖

Keep cool, obey orders and aim low.
  —Confederate General James Longstreet, proclamation to his army
  on the right wing before Richmond, Virginia, June 17, 1862
  [RR 5, 222]

I never had a clear conception of the horrors of war until that
night and the morning. On going round on that battlefield with
a candle searching for my friends I could hear on all sides the
dreadful groans of the wounded and their heart piercing cries
for water and assistance. Friends and foes all together.
  —Confederate soldier A. N. Erskine, letter to his wife, about the
  previous day's battle of Gaines's Mill, Virginia, June 28, 1862
  [JR]

It was thought to be a great thing to charge a battery of artillery
or an earthwork lined with infantry. . . . We were very lavish of
blood in those days.
  —Confederate General D. H. Hill, recalling the many assaults by
  his troops on the Union lines at Gaines's Mill, June 27, 1862
  [BCF]

If I save this army now, I tell you plainly that I owe no thanks to
you or to any other persons in Washington. You have done your
best to sacrifice this army.
  —Union Major General George B. McClellan, letter to President
  Lincoln, after Gaines's Mill, June 28, 1862. (According to E. B.
  Long, in *The Civil War Day by Day*, these "two sentences were
  deleted by War Department staff as unfit for Mr. Lincoln to see.")
  [CWDD, 233]

I, Philip Kearny, an old soldier, enter my solemn protest against
this order for retreat. We ought instead of retreating to follow
up the enemy and take Richmond. And in full view of the
responsibility of such a declaration, I say to you all, such an
order can only be prompted by cowardice or treason.
  —Union General Philip Kearny to his staff, on Commander of the
  Army of the Potomac and Major General George B. McClellan's
  order for retreat after the Battle of Malvern Hill, the last of the
  Seven Days' Battles of the Peninsular Campaign, July 1, 1862
  [CW-1]

❖❖❖

Over five thousand dead and wounded men were on the ground in every attitude of distress. A third of them were dead or dying, but enough were alive and moving to give to the field a singular crawling effect.

> —Union Brevet Major General William W. Averell, recalling the morning after the Battle of Malvern Hill, July 2, 1862
> [BCF]

If at any time you feel able to take the offensive, you are not restrained from doing so.

> —President Abraham Lincoln, note to Major General George B. McClellan, July 4, 1862
> [CW-1]

A declaration of radical views, especially upon slavery, will rapidly disintegrate our present armies. The national forces should not be dispersed in expeditions, posts of occupation, and numerous armies, but should be mainly collected into masses and brought to bear upon the armies of the Confederate States. Those armies thoroughly defeated, the political structure which they support would soon cease to exist.

> —Union Major General George B. McClellan, "Harrison Landing" letter to President Lincoln, July 7, 1862. (McClellan's politically reactionary views on emancipation may have put off Lincoln and his cabinet. McClellan remembers: "I handed him myself, on board the steamer in which [Lincoln] came, the letter of July 7, 1862. He read it in my presence, but made no comments upon it, merely saying, when he had finished it, that he was obliged to me for it, or words to that effect. I do not think that he alluded further to it during his visit, or at any time after that.")
> [MOS, 487]

How can one forgive such enemies as we are contending against? Despoiling us of our property, driving us from our homes and friends and slaying our best citizens on the field are hard crimes to forgive.—At any rate let me have a chance to retaliate and then I can forgive with a better grace.

> —Confederate solider, diary, near Richmond, July 10, 1862
> [JR]

❖❖❖

I am tired of serving fools. God help my country! He alone can save it. It is grating to have to serve under the orders of a man whom I know by experience to be my inferior.

—Union Major General George B. McClellan, letter to his wife, July 20, 1862
[BG 198]

T. G. Freman is Ded and they is Several mor that is Dangerous with the feever. They hev Been 11 Died with the fever in Co A since we left kinston and 2 died that was wounded so you now See that these Big Battles is not as Bad as the fever.

—Confederate soldier J. W. Love, letter home, from near Petersburg, Virginia, August 9, 1862
[JR]

✿

NEW ORLEANS

New Orleans was the largest city in the Confederacy, and of obvious strategic importance, standing as the gateway to the Mississippi River Valley. The Union naval force of twenty-four ships and nineteen mortar boats, led by Admiral David Farragut, captured the city on April 25, and General Benjamin Butler took charge of the administration of New Orleans for the United States Government on May 1.

Imagine all the earthquakes in the world, and all the thunder and lightnings together in a space of two miles, all going off at once. That would be like it.

—Anonymous observer of the mortar bombardments on Forts Jackson and St. Philip, ninety miles south of New Orleans, by Union Admiral David Farragut, in preparation for his fleet's entrance the next week, April 18, 1862. (On April 24, the fleet passed by the forts without damage.)
[CW-1]

❖❖❖

One sparkling, living touch of fire, in manly action for one hour upon each cotton plantation, and the eternal seal of Southern independence is fired and fixed in the great heart of the world.
    —Confederate Major General M. Lovell, General Order No. 17, Camp Moore, Louisiana, May 3, 1862. (Confederate Secretary of War George Randolph, after the fall of New Orleans, instructed Lovell to destroy all the cotton to keep it from the use of the Union.)
    [RR 10, 245]

O if I was only a man! Then I would don the breeches, and slay them with a will! If some Southern women were in the ranks, they would set the men an example they would not blush to follow!
    —Sarah Morgan, diary, May 9, 1862, Baton Rouge, Louisiana
    [WW]

As the officers and soldiers of the United States have been subject to repeated insults from the women (calling themselves ladies) of New Orleans, in return for the most scrupulous non-interference and courtesy on our part, it is ordered that hereafter when any female shall, by word, gesture or movement, insult or show contempt for any officer or soldier of the United States, she shall be regarded and held liable to be treated as a woman of the town plying her avocation.
    —Union Major General Benjamin Butler, Notice, Headquarters Department of the Gulf, New Orleans, General Orders, No. 28, May 15, 1862
    [Harwell, *Confederate Reader*]

Men of the South! Shall our mothers, our wives, our daughters and our sisters be thus outraged by the ruffianly soldiers of the North, to whom is given the right to treat, at their pleasure, the ladies of the South as common harlots? Arouse friends, and drive back from our soil, those infamous invaders of our homes and disturbers of our family ties.
    —Confederate General P. G. T. Beauregard, in response to Butler's General Orders, No. 28, May 15, 1862
    [Harwell, *Confederate Reader*]

———————— ❖❖❖ ————————

Far up the Mississippi River from New Orleans, the walled city of Vicksburg, Mississippi, refused Admiral Farragut's call for surrender.

Mississippians don't know, and refuse to learn, how to surrender to an enemy. If Commodore Farragut or Brigadier General Butler can teach them, let them come and try.

—James L. Autry, military governor and commandant of Vicksburg, Mississippi, letter to Union officer S. Phillips Lee, in reply to the demand of surrender by "the authorities at Vicksburg . . . in advance of the approaching fleet" of Union Admiral David Farragut, May 18, 1862. (Vicksburg learned to surrender on July 4, 1863.)
[RR 5, 426]

*

Observers the world over weighed in on the conflict that threatened to divide the great democratic experiment of America, and in the North and in its armies the feeling gained that slavery was the cause of the war. Great Britain, with mixed feelings of paternal and economic concern, tried to stay out of the war. Had it recognized the Confederacy as a nation, the United States might well have split into two.

The Northerners say that they have given no offence to the Southerners, and that therefore the South is wrong to raise a revolution. The very fact that the North is the North, is an offence to the South.

—Anthony Trollope, British novelist and postal official, who toured the United States from September 1861 to March 1862. He published *North America* on May 19, 1862.
[NA]

Slavery and martial law, in a free country, are altogether incompatible. The persons in these three States—Georgia, Florida and South Carolina—heretofore held as slaves, are therefore declared forever free.

—Union Major General David Hunter, proclamation from headquarters of the Department of the South, Hilton Head, South Carolina, May 9, 1862. (On May 19, President Lincoln declared

❖❖❖

Hunter's proclamation "altogether void." "I further make known, that whether it be competent for me as commander-in-chief of the army and navy to declare the slaves of any State or States free, and whether at any time or in any case, it shall have become a strict necessity indispensable to the maintenance of the government to exercise such supposed power, are questions which, under my responsibility, I reserve to myself, and which I cannot feel justified in leaving to the decision of commanders in the field.")
[RR 5, 123]

You have no friends in Europe. . . . The sentiment in Europe is anti-slavery, and that portion of public opinion which forms, and is represented by the government of Great Britain, is abolition. They will never recognize our independence until our conquering sword hangs dripping over the prostrate heads of the North.
—William L. Yancey, Confederate senator, after his return from lobbying for the Confederacy in England, 1862
[CW-1]

> They say that recognition
> Will the Rebel country save,
> But Johnny Bull and Mister France
> Are 'fraid of Uncle Abe.
—"We'll Fight for Uncle Abe," Union song
[AHD]

Oh Dear it is impossible for me to express my feelings when the fight was over and I saw what was done the tears came then free oh that I never could behold such a sight again to think of it among civilized people killing one another like beasts one would think that the supreme ruler would put a stop to it but we sinned as a nation and must suffer in the flesh as well as spiritually those things we can't account for.
—Confederate soldier S. G. Pryor, letter to his wife, May 18, 1862
[JR]

A year ago we would have considered it impossible to get on for a day without the things that we have been doing without for months. . . . In proportion as we have been a race of haughty,

❖❖❖

indolent, and waited-on people, so now are we ready to do away with all forms and work and wait on ourselves.

—Kate Stone, letter, Brokenburn, Louisiana, May 22, 1862
[CWT: ref: *The Journal of Kate Stone, 1861–1868*, Louisiana State University Press, 1955]

It is very certain that no argument is worth a straw with the Southern rebels but that of the bayonet, and we would be recreant to the cause of liberty on this earth if we did not use it effectually.

—Union Brigadier General Silas Casey, letter to Secretary of War Edwin Stanton, from on board the steamer *Constitution,* May 31, 1862
[RR 5, Doc, 537]

✿

STONEWALL JACKSON AND THE
SHENANDOAH VALLEY CAMPAIGN

The great Confederate General Thomas J. "Stonewall" Jackson was a deeply religious man and yet a fierce and passionate warrior. The former professor at Virginia Military Institute was relentless with his men, and his two-month campaign in the Shenandoah Valley was a strategic diversion, drawing attention and forces from McClellan's army on the Virginia Peninsula.

You appear much concerned at my attacking *on Sunday.* I was greatly concerned, too; but I felt it my duty to do it, in consideration of the ruinous effects that might result from postponing the battle until morning. So far as I can see, my course was a wise one; the best that I could do under the circumstances, though very distasteful to my feelings; and I hope and pray to our Heavenly Father that I may never again be circumstanced as on that day. I believed that so far as our troops were concerned, necessity and mercy both called for the battle.

—Confederate General Stonewall Jackson, letter to his wife, from Manassas, Virginia, April 11, 1862
[TJJ]

❖❖❖

We can get along without anything but food and ammunition. The road to glory cannot be followed with much baggage.

> —Confederate General Richard Ewell, in pursuit of Union General Nathaniel Banks's forces, during the Shenandoah Valley Campaign, May 21, 1862
> [O.R. 1, Vol 12, Pt. 3, 890]

By God, sir! I will not retreat. We have more to fear from the opinions of our friends than the bayonets of our enemies!

> —Union General Nathaniel Banks, to Colonel George H. Gordon, who suggested retreat after the loss to Stonewall Jackson's Army of the Valley at Front Royal, Virginia, May 23, 1862. (Within hours Banks sensibly called for a retreat to Winchester.)
> [CW-1]

Colonel, I yield to no man in sympathy for the gallant men under my command, but I am obliged to sweat them tonight that I may save their blood tomorrow.

> —Confederate General Stonewall Jackson to an officer who had suggested rest for their fatigued soldiers during the pursuit of Union General Nathaniel Banks's army, near Winchester, Virginia, May 24, 1862
> [CW-1]

No one could love the man for himself. He seems to be cut off from his fellow men and to commune with his own spirit only, or with spirits of which we know not.

> —Confederate officer, letter home about Stonewall Jackson
> [CW-1]

You must not expect long letters from me in such busy times as these, but always believe your husband never forgets his little darling.

> —Confederate General Stonewall Jackson, letter to his wife, from Mount Jackson, Virginia, during the Shenandoah Valley Campaign, June 2, 1862
> [TJJ]

❖❖❖

Give me ten thousand men, and I would be in Washington
tomorrow.
—Confederate General Stonewall Jackson
[CW-1]

He who does not see the hand of God in his is blind, sir. Blind!
—Confederate General Stonewall Jackson to General Richard
Ewell, having routed General John Fremont at the end of Jackson's
successful Shenandoah Valley Campaign, June 9, 1862
[CW-1]

I had rather be a private in such an army than a field officer in
any other army.
—Confederate soldier in "Jackson's Brigade," letter, June 9, 1862
[CWDD, 225]

Moses took forty years to lead the Israelites through the wilder-
ness, with manna to feed them on; "Old Jack" would have
double-quicked through it on half-rations in three days.
—Confederate joke, about General Stonewall Jackson on the
Shenandoah Valley Campaign, June 1862
[TJJ]

✿

*By mid-year, the Union forces continued to reclaim seceded ter-
ritory, but they were not defeating or reducing the Confederate
forces. Lincoln called for more soldiers, and in pursuit of a more
aggressive leadership, on July 11 named Henry Halleck general
in chief of all armies, who promptly bypassed McClellan by
naming John Pope to lead the Army of Virginia on its next campaign. Ulysses S. Grant, meanwhile, assumed command of the
Army of the Tennessee and Mississippi.*

Listen, young heroes! your country is calling!
Time strikes the hour for the brave and the true!
Now, while the foremost are fighting and falling,
Fill up the ranks that opened for you!
—"An Appeal," Oliver Wendell Holmes, 1862
[RR 5]

❖❖❖

You have called us, and we're coming, by Richmond's bloody
tide
To lay us down, for Freedom's sake, our brothers' bones
beside,
Or from foul treason's savage grasp to wrench the murderous
blade,
And in the face of foreign foes its fragments to parade.
Six hundred thousand loyal men and true have gone before:
We are coming, Father Abraham, three hundred thousand
more!

—"Three Hundred Thousand More," by abolitionist James Sloan
Gibbons (music by Stephen Foster), July 1862. (". . . I have decided
to call into the service an additional three hundred thousand men,"
President Lincoln wrote in reply to the offer of Union governors to
supply all the men he needed "to speedily crush the rebellion," July
1, 1862.)
[RR 5]

> The Irish boys are bold and brave,
> The Irish boys are true;
> They love the dear old stars and stripes,
> The spangled field of blue.

—"The Irish Boys," by "C.M.," 1862
[RR 5]

After accepting several men over forty-five years of age, and several infants, such as a man like me could whip a dozen of, I was
rejected because I had the honesty to acknowledge I was more
than forty-five years of age. The mustering officer was a very
good-looking man, about thirty-five years old, but I guess I can
run faster and jump higher than he; also take him down, whip
him, endure more hardships, and kill three rebels to his one.

—James Leonard, of Upper Gilmanton, New Hampshire, rejected
as a volunteer, summer 1862
[RR 6, Poetry, 9]

We must free the slaves or be ourselves subdued. The slaves
were undeniably an element of strength to those who had their

❖❖❖

service, and we must decide whether that element should be with us or against us.

—President Abraham Lincoln, speaking to Secretary of the Navy Gideon Welles, July 13, 1862. (On July 22, Lincoln broached to his cabinet his intention to issue an emancipation proclamation.) [BCF]

The strongest position a soldier should desire to occupy is one from which he can most easily advance against the enemy. Let us study the probable lines of retreat of our opponents, and leave our own to take care of themselves. Let us look before us, and not behind. Success and glory are in the advance; disaster and shame lurk in the rear.

—Union Major General John Pope, address "To the Officers and Soldiers of the Army of Virginia," Headquarters of the Army of Virginia, Washington, D.C., July 14, 1862. (Newly made commander of this army, having had success in the West, Pope scolded the troops for their defensive-mindedness, saying, "I presume I have been called here to pursue the same system"—i.e., staying out of "a defensive attitude.") [UR; RR]

I just took the short cut and got there first with the most men.

—Confederate General Nathan Bedford Forrest, explaining to cavalry raider John H. Morgan how he had taken federal stores in spite of Union troops surrounding him, summer 1862 [CWT: ref: *Reminiscences of General Basil W. Duke*, 1911, 344]

*

On President Lincoln

It took some time for President Lincoln to be appreciated. Many civic leaders and politicians (not to mention General George B. McClellan) condescended to him.

Not a spark of genius has he; not an element for leadership. Not one particle of heroic enthusiasm.

—Preacher Henry Ward Beecher of Brooklyn, speech, 1862 [CW-1]

❖❖❖

He may be honest—nobody cares whether the tortoise is honest or not. He has neither insight, nor prevision, nor decision.
    —Wendell Phillips, abolitionist, of Boston, speech, summer 1862
    [CW-1]

We, Catholics, and a vast majority of our brave troops in the field, have not the slightest idea of carrying on a war that costs so much blood and treasure just to gratify a clique of Abolitionists in the North.
    —Archbishop John Hughes of New York, letter to Union Secretary of War Cameron, summer 1862
    [CW-1/ John Hassard, *Life of the Most Reverend John Hughes*, 1866, 437]

Money you have expended without limit, and blood poured out like water. Defeat, debt, taxation, and sepulchers—these are your only trophies.
    —Congressional Representative Clement L. Vallandigham, Democrat of Ohio, to the House Republicans, about the Lincoln administration
    [CW-2]

I expect to maintain this contest until successful, or till I die, or am conquered, or my term expires, or Congress or the country forsake me.
    —President Abraham Lincoln, summer 1862
    [CW-1]

The Government seems determined to apply the guillotine to all unsuccessful generals. It seems rather hard to do this where the general is not in fault, but perhaps with us now, as in the French Revolution, some harsh measures are required.
    —Union Major General Henry Halleck, letter to Major General Horacio Wright, commander at Louisville, August 25, 1862
    [O.R. Ser 1, Vol 16, Pt. 2, 421]

He has a kind of shrewdness and common sense, mother wit, and slipshod, low-leveled honesty, that made him a good Western

❖❖❖

jury lawyer. But he is an unutterable calamity to us where he is.
Only the army can save us.
—Richard Dana, author and Massachusetts Republican, on
President Lincoln
[CW-2]

❖

SECOND BULL RUN CAMPAIGN AND ANTIETAM

*In an attempt to draw Robert E. Lee's Army of Northern
Virginia away from Richmond while at the same time protecting
Washington, D.C., Union General John Pope's new Army of
Virginia set out in mid-July. While McClellan's army remained
in place before him, Lee sent Stonewall Jackson and A. P. Hill to
meet Pope. When McClellan withdrew troops to reinforce Pope,
Lee and General James Longstreet reinforced Jackson's. Union
and Confederate armies then battled again near Manassas, the
site of a Confederate victory in 1861, and "Second Bull Run"
proved to be another decisive Confederate victory. Lee now set
out on his first "invasion" of the North, crossing into Maryland.
The Battle of Sharpsburg, or Antietam, on September 17, was
"the bloodiest single day of the war." Lee's army, though not
defeated, was turned away by McClellan's, and retreated into
Virginia, which amounted to a Union "victory" that allowed
President Lincoln the opportunity to announce his preliminary
Emancipation Proclamation.*

. . . we must think of the living and of those who are to come
after us, and see that, with God's blessing, we transmit to them
the freedom we have enjoyed. What is life without honor?
Degradation is worse than death. It is necessary that you should
be at your post immediately. Join me tomorrow morning.
—Confederate General Stonewall Jackson, at Harper's Ferry,
Virginia, letter to an officer requesting an extended furlough with
his grieving family, August 2, 1862
[TJJ]

———————❖❖❖———————

I don't like Jackson's movements—he will suddenly appear when least expected.

> —Union Major General George B. McClellan, telegram to Major General Henry Halleck, on Confederate General Stonewall Jackson, during the Second Bull Run Campaign, August 14, 1862
> [CW-1]

You have my hat and plume. I have your best coat. I have the honor to propose a cartel for a fair exchange of the prisoners.

> —Confederate Major General J. E. B. Stuart, note to Union Major General John Pope, after Stuart's capture of Pope's headquarters wagon, August 22, 1862
> [CWT]

Before this war is over, I intend to be a major general or a corpse.

> —Confederate Brigadier General Isaac Trimble, setting out for Manassas on the Second Bull Run Campaign, August 26, 1862. (The 60-year-old was appointed major general in April 1863 and lived until 1888.)
> [CW-1]

Pope has his headquarters in the saddle, and McDowell his head in a basket.

> —Disgruntled Union soldiers, on Generals John Pope and Irvin McDowell, about the first of whom it was also said "his headquarters are where his hindquarters should be," while McDowell was conspicuous for wearing a large woven hat for shade, Second Bull Run Campaign, August 28, 1862
> [CW-1]

I don't care for John Pope one pinch of owl dung.

> —Union General Samuel Sturgis, commander of "Sturgis's Brigade," at Second Bull Run, on Major General John Pope, the commander of the Army of the Potomac
> [CW-3]

"General, this day has been won by nothing but stark and stern fighting."

❖❖❖

"No. It has been won by nothing but the blessing and protection of Providence."
> —Confederate General Stonewall Jackson's medical director in conversation with Jackson, after the first day's battle at Second Bull Run, August 29, 1862
> [CW-1]

When garbage lies everywhere in the company streets, and the air has a noisome odor both within and without the tents, we have found, also that the men are dirty, ragged and sickly—their muskets are rusty and out of order—they are insubordinate, mutinous, without drill and without discipline. They have no *esprit de corps*—no self respect—no manliness—no courage; and they will not fight. These are the links which compose the chain. Dirt at one end, and cowardice at the other—commencing in the camp at Alexandria, and ending in the rout upon the plains of Manassas.
> —Union medical director
> [DB, 197]

I cannot but feel that giving command to McClellan is equivalent to giving Washington to the rebels.
> —Union Secretary of the Treasury Salmon P. Chase to fellow cabinet members, on the reappointment of Major General George B. McClellan as commander in chief, August 31, 1862. (McClellan saw it differently, writing on September 5 to his wife: "Again I have been called upon to save the country.")
> [CW-1]

McClellan is an intelligent engineer and officer, but not a commander to lead a great army in the field. To attack or advance with energy and power is not in him; to fight is not his forte. I sometimes fear his heart is not earnest in the cause; yet I do not entertain the thought that he is unfaithful. . . . he likes show, parade, and power. Wishes to outgeneral the Rebels, but not to kill and destroy them.
> —Union Secretary of the Navy Gideon Welles, diary, on McClellan's reappointment as commander in chief
> [BG 193]

❖❖❖

My God, boys, you know who you have killed? You have shot the most gallant officer in the United States Army. This is Phil Kearny, who lost his arm in the Mexican War.

—Confederate General Stonewall Jackson, on Union Major General Philip Kearny, who had mistakenly ridden over to the Confederate lines at Second Bull Run, September 1, 1862
[CWT: ref: Thomas Kearny, *General Philip Kearny, Battle Soldier of Five Wars,* 1937]

This army today achieved on the plains of Manassas a signal victory over combined forces of Generals McClellan and Pope. . . . We mourn the loss of our gallant dead in every conflict, yet our gratitude to Almighty God for his mercies rises higher and higher each day. To Him and to the valor of our troops a nation's gratitude is due.

—Confederate General Robert E. Lee, letter to Confederate President Jefferson Davis, September 1, 1862
[CW-1]

> Pope and McDowell fighting for a town,
> Up jumped Lee and knocked them both down.

—Confederate nursery rhyme on Union generals, after Second Bull Run
[JR]

Give me a victory and I will give you a poem, but I am now clear down to the bottom of the well, where I see the Truth too near to make verses of.

—James Russell Lowell, poet, letter to his publisher, summer 1862
[CW-1]

We cannot afford to be idle, and though weaker than our opponents in men and military equipments, must endeavor to harass them if we cannot destroy them.

—Confederate General Robert E. Lee, letter from Manassas to Confederate President Jefferson Davis, September 3, 1862. (Lee now set off on the Antietam Campaign.)
[CW-1]

❖❖❖

I agree with you that the time is come for offering mediation to the United States Government, with a view to recognition of the independence of the Confederates. I agree further that, in case of failure, we ought ourselves to recognize the Southern States as an independent State.
  —British Foreign Minister Earl Russell, reply to Lord Palmerston's considering Great Britain's recognition of the Confederate States of America, after hearing of Second Bull Run and that Lee's army had entered Maryland, September 17, 1862
  [EHA]

He is an able general, but a very cautious one. His enemies among his own people think him too much so. His army is in a very demoralized and chaotic condition, and will not be prepared for offensive operations (or he will not think it so) for three or four weeks. Before that time I hope to be on the Susquehanna.
  —Confederate General Robert E. Lee, in conversation with General John G. Walker, about Union Major General George B. McClellan, September 1862. (Lee was briefing Walker on "Special Orders 191," the Antietam Campaign maneuver that would strike the first blow in his invasion of the North.)
  [CW-1]

Here is a paper with which if I cannot whip Bobby Lee I will be willing to go home.
  —Union Major General George B. McClellan, to General John Gibbon, on reading "Special Orders 191," Confederate General Robert E. Lee's battle plans of September 9, 1862, found by two Union soldiers. McClellan, however, was worried that the papers might have been left as a trick, and did not take full advantage. (By September 13, Lee discovered McClellan knew his plans, and pulled his divided forces together. On September 18, Lee withdrew his army to Virginia, and the Union, having turned the Confederate forces away at Antietam with terrible casualties on both sides, claimed victory.)
  [BCF]

❖❖❖

Men, you are about to engage in battle. You have never disgraced your state; I hope you won't this time. If any man runs I want the file closers to shoot him; if they don't, I shall myself. That's all I have to say.

—Union Colonel E. E. Cross, at Antietam, September 16, 1862
[DE, 133]

We are through for tonight, gentlemen, but tomorrow we fight the battle that will decide the fate of the republic.

—Union General Joseph Hooker, to his officers, having set up his corps' lines, September 16, 1862, after some skirmishing between his and rebel troops. (Hooker was shot in the foot the next morning.)
[RR 5, Doc, 467]

The rebel dead lay in winrows and both our men and the rebels lay in every direction. . . . We were glad to march over the field at night for we could not see the horrible sights so well.

—Union soldier Cyrus Stone, letter to his parents after the Battle of Antietam
[BY]

I had no shoes. I tried to barefoot, but somehow my feet wouldn't callous. They just kept bleeding. I found it so hard to keep up that though I had the heart of a patriot, I began to feel I didn't have patriotic feet. Of course, I could have crawled on my hands and knees, but then my hands would have got so sore I couldn't have fired my rifle.

—Confederate soldier, asked by his officer how it was he had missed the Battle of Antietam, September 17, 1862
[CWT: ref: Helen Dorich Longstreet, *In the Path of Lee's "Old War Horse,"* 1917]

Our victory was complete, and the disorganized rebel army has rapidly returned to Virginia, its dreams of "invading Pennsylvania" dissipated for ever. I feel some little pride in having, with a

❖❖❖

beaten and demoralized army, defeated Lee so utterly and saved the North so completely.

—Union Major General George B. McClellan, letter to his wife, from a camp near Sharpsburg, Virginia, September 20, 1862. (McClellan's self-congratulatory assessment of the Battle of Antietam was not shared by most of his peers, opponents, and superiors.)
[BG]

✿

PRELIMINARY EMANCIPATION PROCLAMATION

There was surprise, shock, outrage, and joy in the North after President Lincoln issued his preliminary emancipation proclamation on September 22, 1862. Until his announcement of it, Lincoln had argued in public, rather disingenuously, against its immediate likelihood. Some Union soldiers and officers declared they had not signed up for and would not fight for this cause (very few quit after all) while the proclamation made others feel justified in their sacrifice of life and limb. In any case the public reaction—taking the proclamation as the ultimate and impending end of slavery in the country—went beyond Lincoln's stated points, which granted emancipation as of January 1, 1863, but only to those slaves in seceded states. The Confederacy, on the other hand, considered Lincoln's proclamation as evidence of what Southern leaders had been saying all along, that the purpose of the war was to end slavery. The Union began recruiting African-Americans for the army.

> In vain the bells of war shall ring
> Of triumphs and revenges,
> While still is spared the evil thing
> That severs and estranges.
> But blest the ear
> That yet shall hear
> The jubilant bell
> That rings the knell
> Of Slavery forever!

—John Greenleaf Whittier, from the poem "Ein feste Burg ist unser Gott"
[CWP]

———❖❖❖———

We complain that the Union cause has suffered . . . from mistaken deference to Rebel slavery. . . . All attempts to put down the Rebellion and at the same time uphold its inciting cause are preposterous and futile.

—Horace Greeley, "The Prayer of Twenty Millions," editorial, *New York Tribune*, August 19, 1862
[CWDD, 253]

If there be those who would not save the Union unless they could at the same time destroy slavery, I do not agree with them. My paramount object in this struggle is to save the Union, and is not either to save or destroy slavery. If I could save the Union without freeing any slave, I would do it; and if I could save it by freeing all the slaves, I would do it; and if I could save it by freeing some and leaving others alone, I would also do that. What I do about slavery and the colored race, I do because I believe it helps to save the Union; and what I forbear, I forbear because I do not believe it would help to save the Union.

—President Abraham Lincoln, "Executive Mansion" reply to Horace Greeley's "The Prayer of Twenty Millions," August 22, 1862
[CW-1]

The will of God prevails. In great contests each party claims to act in accordance with the will of God. Both *may* be, and one *must* be, wrong. God cannot be *for* and *against* the same thing at the same time. In the present civil war it is quite possible that God's purpose is something different from the purpose of either party—and yet the human instrumentalities, working just as they do, are of the best adaptation to effect His purpose.

—President Abraham Lincoln, "Meditation on the Divine Will," on or about September 2, 1862
[CW-1]

The slave oligarchy has organized the most unnatural, perfidious and formidable rebellion known to history. It has professedly established an independent government on the avowed basis of slavery, admitting that the Federal Union was constituted to conserve and promote liberty. . . . We cannot expect God to save a nation that clings to its sin. This is too fearful an hour to insult God, or to deceive ourselves. . . . We urge you, therefore, as the head of this Christian nation, from considerations of moral principle, and, as the only means of preserving the Union, to proclaim, without delay, NATIONAL EMANCIPATION.

   —L. B. Otis, Chairman, and E. W. Blatchford, Secretary, "Memorial of the Public Meeting of the Christian Men of Chicago," letter to President Lincoln, September 7, 1862
[UR]

Would my word free the slaves, when I cannot even enforce the Constitution in the rebel states?

   —President Abraham Lincoln, to a group of ministers from Chicago, September 13, 1862
[CW-1]

When the rebel army was at Frederick, I determined, as soon as it should be driven out of Maryland, to issue a proclamation of emancipation, such as I thought most likely to be useful. I said nothing to anyone; but I made the promise to myself and to my Maker. The rebel army is now driven out, and I am going to fulfill that promise.

   —President Abraham Lincoln, to his cabinet, September 22, 1862
[CW-1]

. . . on the first day of January in the year of our Lord, one thousand eight hundred and sixty-three, all persons held as slaves within any state, or designated part of a state, the people whereof shall then be in rebellion against the United States shall be then, thenceforward, and forever free . . .

   —President Abraham Lincoln, "Preliminary Emancipation Proclamation," September 22, 1862
[GS]

❖❖❖

THE CONFEDERATE INVASION OF KENTUCKY

Before the Emancipation Proclamation and simultaneous with the Manassas and Antietam campaigns in the East, in the Western theater of the war, the Confederacy attempted to exploit what it hoped was the pro-Southern sympathy of Kentucky, which had wavered at the outbreak of secession but had remained part of the Union. Generals Braxton Bragg and Edmund Kirby Smith led the invasions, which resulted in initial success for Smith against Union forces at Richmond, Kentucky, on August 30. In early October, Bragg's forces were defeated by General Don Carlos Buell's at the Battle of Perryville, and forced to retreat into east Tennessee, thus ending the Confederacy's reestablishment in Kentucky.

The enemy is before us, devastating our fair country, imprisoning our old and venerated men (even the ministers of God), insulting our women, and desecrating our altars. It is our proud lot to be assigned the duty of punishing and driving forth these deluded men, led by desperate adventurers and goaded on by Abolition demagogues and demons. Let us but deserve success and an offended Deity will certainly assure it.

—Confederate General Braxton Bragg, General Order, read to his troops of the Army of Tennessee in Chattanooga, before setting off for an invasion of Kentucky, August 28, 1862
[CW-1]

Let no one make you believe we come as invaders, to coerce your will or to exercise control over your soil. Far from it. . . . We come to test the truth of what we believe to be a foul aspersion, that Kentuckians willingly join the attempt to subjugate us and to deprive us of our prosperity, our liberty, and our dearest rights.

—Confederate General Edmund Kirby Smith, proclamation to the people of Kentucky, August 1862
[CW-1]

If you prefer Federal rule, show it by your frowns and we shall return whence we came. If you choose rather to come within the folds of our brotherhood, then cheer us with the smiles of

❖❖❖

your women and lend your willing hands to secure you in your
heritage of liberty.
   —Confederate General Braxton Bragg's proclamation to the people
   of Kentucky, from Glascow, Kentucky, September 14, 1862
   [O.R., Ser 1, Vol 16, Pt. 2, 822]

The Kentuckians are slow and backward in rallying to our standard. Their hearts are evidently with us, but their blue-grass and
fat cattle are against us.
   —Confederate General E. Kirby Smith, in Lexington, Kentucky,
   letter to General Braxton Bragg, late September, 1862. (Frustrated
   by his inability to recruit Kentuckians into the Confederacy, Bragg
   wrote his wife, "Why should I stay with my handful of brave
   Southern men to fight for cowards who skulked about in the dark to
   say to us, 'We are with you. Only whip these fellows out of our country and let us see you can protect us, and we will join you'?")
   [CW-1]

About half past five in the morning of the ninth, I dropped—I
could do no more. I went out by myself and leaning against a
fence, I wept like a child. And all that day I was so unnerved that
if anyone asked me about the regiment, I could make no reply
without tears. Having taken off my shirt to make bandages, I
took a severe cold.
   —Union surgeon, after working all night at the Battle of Perryville,
   Kentucky, October 8, 1862
   [CWM, 124]

                              ✿

*In the fall of 1862, after its retreat from Kentucky and the failed
invasion of Maryland, the Confederacy saw its exultation in
the victories of the summer dissolve. President Lincoln's
Emancipation Proclamation now seemed to preclude foreign
recognition of the Confederacy.*

We may have our own opinions about slavery; we may be for or
against the South; but there is no doubt that Jefferson Davis and
other leaders of the South have made an army. They are mak-

———◆◆◆———

ing, it appears, a navy. And they have made what is more than either; they have made a nation.

—William E. Gladstone, Chancellor of the Exchequer, of the British cabinet, speech at Newcastle, England, October 7, 1862. (The Foreign Secretary, Lord John Russell, scolded Gladstone for seeming to recognize the Confederacy as a nation: ". . . for that step I think the Cabinet is not prepared.")
[ELCW, 186]

While the General is wielding the sword of the flesh, I trust that I am using the sword of the Spirit. He is fighting the rebels, and I am fighting the spirits of darkness. There is this difference: he is fighting with Price, while I am fighting without price.

—Bishop Sylvester Rosecrans, answering a remark at a dinner about the "very different callings" of his and his brother's, Union General William Rosecrans, who was facing Confederate General Sterling Price in Mississippi, October 8, 1862
[RR 7]

Missus, we're even now; you sold all my children; the Lord took all yours; not one left to bury either of us; now I forgive you.

—"An old slave mother," to her mistress, after a battle in which the mistress's last son, a Confederate colonel, had been killed
[RR 7, Poetry, 17]

If I ever lose my patriotism, and the "secesh" spirit dies out, then you may know the "Commissary" is at fault. Corn meal mixed with water and tough beef three times a day will knock the "Brave Volunteer" under quicker than Yankee bullets.

—Confederate soldier Robert W. Banks, letter home, October 22, 1862
[JR]

The enemy is superior to us in everything but courage, and therefore it is quite certain, if the war is to go on until exhaustion overtake the one side or the other side, that we shall be the first to be exhausted.

—Confederate Senator Herschel V. Johnson, of Georgia, asked by a friend if he had "confidence in the success of the Southern Confederacy," late October 1862
[RR 7]

❖❖❖

ABRAHAM LINCOLN AND GEORGE B. MCCLELLAN

The President and McClellan continued their testy relationship until Lincoln could not bear McClellan's delays any longer. One annoyance, famous though inconsequential, was the Confederate cavalry General J. E. B. Stuart's second "ride 'round McClellan" October 9–12. Lincoln ordered McClellan replaced as commander in chief by General Ambrose Burnside. Both McClellan and Lincoln seemed emotionally relieved by the decision. In 1864, McClellan became Lincoln's primary challenger for the presidency.

Our people generally feel that, bad as they are, they are not as bad as they might be.

—Union Colonel A. K. McClure, on the Confederate cavalry raid led by J. E. B. Stuart and its takeover of Chambersburg, Pennsylvania, during Stuart's second "ride 'round McClellan," October 10, 1862
[BG 234]

If we oppose force to force we cannot win, for their resources are greater than ours. We must substitute *esprit* for numbers. Therefore I strive to inculcate in my men the spirit of the chase.

—Confederate Major General J. E. B. Stuart. (The famous James Ewell Brown Stuart was killed in a fight against Union General Philip Sheridan's cavalry two years later.)
[CW-1]

Three times round and out is the rule in baseball. Stuart has been round twice around McClellan. The third time, by the rules of the game, he must surrender.

—President Abraham Lincoln, to Adams S. Hill, *New York Tribune*, on Confederate Major General J. E. B. Stuart, who had twice led his cavalry around Major General George McClellan's Army of the Potomac, October 1862
[RWAL, 256]

You remember my speaking to you of what I called your overcautiousness. Are you not overcautious when you assume that you can

❖❖❖

not do what the enemy is constantly doing? Should you not claim
to be at least his equal in prowess, and act upon the claim?

> —President Abraham Lincoln, letter to Major General George B.
> McClellan, October 13, 1862. Lincoln urged McClellan to appreci-
> ate his army's advantages after Antietam and immediately attack.
> [UR]

I have just read your dispatch about sore-tongued and fatigued
horses. Will you pardon me for asking what the horses of your
army have done since the battle of Antietam that fatigues anything?

> —President Abraham Lincoln, complete telegram to Major
> General George B. McClellan, October 25, 1862. (Two days later
> Lincoln apologized in a letter and explained his impatience with
> "five weeks of total inaction of the Army.")
> [CW-1/WW]

There is an immobility here that exceeds all that any man can
conceive of. It requires the lever of Archimedes to move this
inert mass.

> —Union Major General Henry Halleck, letter to Hamilton
> Gamble, about Major General George B. McClellan's reluctance to
> move his Army of the Potomac into an attack on the Confederate
> Army of Northern Virginia, October 30, 1862
> [BCF]

If he had a million men he would swear the enemy has two millions, and then he would sit down in the mud and yell for three.

> —Secretary of War Edwin Stanton, on Major General George B.
> McClellan
> [AHD]

I said I would remove him if he let Lee's army get away from
him, and I must do so. He has got the "slows," Mr. Blair.

> —President Abraham Lincoln, to General Francis Blair, on Major
> General George B. McClellan, November 7, 1862
> [CW-1]

❖❖❖

By direction of the President of the United States, it is ordered that Major General McClellan be relieved from the command of the Army of the Potomac, and that Major General Burnside take the command of that army.

—President Abraham Lincoln, orders to Major General Henry Halleck, which McClellan received November 7, 1862
[MOS, 650]

That I must have made many mistakes I cannot deny. I do not see any great blunders—but no one can judge of himself. Our consolation must be that we have tried to do what was right; if we have failed, it was not our fault.

—Union Major General George B. McClellan, letter to his wife, on being relieved of his command, camp near Rectortown, Virginia, November 7, 1862
[MOS, 660]

An order of the President devolves upon Major General Burnside the command of this Army. In parting from you I cannot express the love and gratitude I bear to you. As an army you have grown up under my care. In you I have never found doubt or coldness. The battles you have fought under my command will proudly live in our nation's history.

—Union Major General George B. McClellan, farewell address to the "Officers and Soldiers of the Army of the Potomac," camp near Rectortown, Virginia, November 7, 1862
[MOS, 653]

We always understood each other so well. I fear they may continue to make those changes till they find someone whom I don't understand.

—Confederate General Robert E. Lee, remarking on Union Major General McClellan's removal as commander of the Army of the Potomac, November 10, 1862.
[CW-1]

❖❖❖

THE BATTLE OF FREDERICKSBURG

Where General George B. McClellan had been cautiously leading his Army of the Potomac toward Richmond, his replacement, General Ambrose Burnside, drove from the east to cross the army at the Rappahannock River to Fredericksburg. This crossing took so long to prepare, however, that Confederate General Robert E. Lee had plenty of time to set up his forces to oppose him. Two days after the disastrous battle on December 13, Burnside decided to retreat.

General, if you put every man now on the other side of the Potomac in that field to approach me over that same line, and give me plenty of ammunition, I will kill them all before they reach my line.

—Confederate General James Longstreet to General Robert E. Lee, at Marye's Heights, Fredericksburg, Virginia, December 13, 1862. (More than ten percent of the Union soldiers at Fredericksburg were killed or wounded on this day.)
[CW-2]

Finding that I had lost as many men as my orders required me to lose, I suspended the attack.

—Union General Joseph Hooker, official report on the Battle of Fredericksburg, December 13, 1862
[CW-2]

They went as they came—in the night. They suffered heavily as far as battle went, but it did not go far enough to satisfy me.

—Stonewall Jackson, letter to his wife, after defeating the Union forces under General Ambrose Burnside at Fredericksburg, December 13, 1862
[TJJ]

> Burnside, Burnside, whither dost thou wander
> Up stream, down stream, like a crazy gander.

—Anonymous verse
[JR]

❖❖❖

It can hardly be in human nature for men to show more valor, or generals to manifest less judgment, than were perceptible on our side that day.

—*Cincinnati Daily Commercial,* on the Union defeat at Fredericksburg, December 13, 1862
[CW-2; WW]

It is well that war is so terrible; we should grow too fond of it.

—Confederate General Robert E. Lee, to General James Longstreet, at Fredericksburg, December 13, 1862. (The Union forces suffered more than twice the losses of the Confederates at this battle.)
[CWT: ref: *Southern Magazine,* 1874]

Don't you see that your system feeds upon itself? You cannot fill the places of these men. Your troops do wonders, but every time at a cost you cannot afford.

—Anonymous "British observer" of Confederate General Robert E. Lee's army, after Fredericksburg
[CW-2]

We must do more than defeat their armies. We must destroy them.

—Stonewall Jackson, after Fredericksburg, December 1862
[CW-2]

Lord! What a scramble there'll be for arms and legs, when we old boys come out of our graves, on Judgment Day: wonder if we shall get our own again? If we do, my leg will have to tramp from Fredericksburg, my arm from here, I suppose, and meet my body, wherever it may be.

—A Union sergeant, to nurse and author Louisa May Alcott, in a Washington, D.C., hospital after the Battle of Fredericksburg, December 1862
[UR]

Well, 'twas my fust, you see, so I ain't ashamed to say I was a trifle flustered in the beginnin', there was such an all-fired racket; for ef there's anything I do spleen agin, it's noise. But when my

❖❖❖

mate, Eph Sylvester, caved, with a bullet through his head, I got mad, and pitched in, licketty cut.

—A Union soldier from New Hampshire, to nurse and author Louisa May Alcott, in a Washington, D.C., hospital after the Battle of Fredericksburg, December 1862
[UR]

But what a cruel thing is war; to separate and destroy families and friends, and mar the purest joys and happiness God has granted us in this world; to fill our hearts with hatred instead of love for our neighbors, and to devastate the fair face of this beautiful world. I pray that, on this day when only peace and good-will are preached to mankind, better thoughts may fill the hearts of our enemies and turn them to peace.

—Confederate Major General Stonewall Jackson, letter to his wife, December 25, 1862
[TJJ]

❂

The year was ending with the North and South realizing how much devastation this war had caused and would continue to cause—and at the same time, with the Emancipation Proclamation on the verge of becoming law, all sensed that the social order would never again be the same.

Without slavery the rebellion could never have existed; without slavery it could not continue.

—President Abraham Lincoln, annual message to Congress, December 1, 1862
[GS]

In *giving* freedom to the *slave*, we *assure* freedom to the *free*—honorable alike in what we give, and what we preserve.

—President Abraham Lincoln, annual message to Congress, December 1, 1862
[GS]

———— ❖❖❖ ————

All equally see in the convulsion in America an era in the history of the world, out of which must come in the end a general recognition of the right of mankind to the produce of their labor and the pursuit of happiness.

—Charles Francis Adams, letter to his son, Charles Francis Adams, Jr., from Mount Felix, Walton on Thames, England, December 25, 1862
[CAL, 220–221]

We cannot change the hearts of the people of the South, but we can make war so terrible that they will realize the fact that however brave and gallant and devoted to their country, still they are mortal and should exhaust all peaceful remedies before they fly to war.

—Union General William Tecumseh Sherman, letter to Major General Ulysses S. Grant, 1862
[CW-1]

We are not engaged in a conflict for conquest, or for aggrandizement, or for the settlement of a point of international law. The question for you to decide is, Will you be slaves or will you be independent? . . . After what has happened during the last two years, my only wonder is that we consented to live for so long a time in association with such miscreants and have loved so much a government rotten to the core. Were it ever to be proposed again to enter into a Union with such a people, I could not more consent to do it than to trust myself in a den of thieves.

—Confederate President Jefferson Davis, speech to Mississippi state legislature, December 26, 1862
[CW-2]

"Put not your trust in princes," and rest not your hopes on foreign nations. This war is ours; we must fight it out ourselves; and I feel some pride in knowing that so far we have done it without the good will of anybody.

—Confederate President Jefferson Davis, speech before the legislature of Mississippi, December 26, 1862
[RR 6]

The spirit of enlistment is thrice dead. Enthusiasm has expired to a cold pile of damp ashes. Defeats, retreats, sufferings, dangers, magnified by spiritless helplessness and an unchangeable conviction that our army is in the hands of ignorant and feeble commanders, are rapidly producing a sense of settled despair.

—Confederate Senator James Phelan, letter to President Jefferson Davis, December 1862
[CW-2]

Heartily do we congratulate you and your country on this humane and righteous course. We assume that you cannot now stop short of a complete uprooting of slavery.

—The Citizens of Manchester, England, assembled at Free-Trade Hall, address to President Lincoln, December 31, 1862. (President Lincoln answered, thanking them, on January 19, 1863.)
[RR 6]

✿

STONES RIVER (MURFREESBORO)

In Tennessee, the last major battle of the year continued into the new year. After the Battle of Perryville in October, Confederate General Bragg set up in Murfreesboro, Tennessee. Meanwhile, the Union reorganized its forces in eastern Tennessee as the Army of the Cumberland, with General William Rosecrans in command. After much prodding from Washington, D.C., Rosecrans moved his force from Nashville to attack Bragg near Stones River. While the Confederates won the battle, Rosecrans's army was able to hold its position around Murfreesboro, with Bragg's army retreating south on January 3, 1863.

I need no other stimulus to make me do my duty than the knowledge of what it is. To threats of removal or the like I must be permitted to say that I am insensible.

—Union General William Rosecrans, commander of the Army of the Cumberland, to Major General Henry Halleck, December 4, 1862, after Halleck wrote him that "If you remain one more week in Nashville, I cannot prevent your removal."
[CW-2]

———————— ❖❖❖ ————————

Be cool—I need not ask you to be brave. Keep ranks, do not throw away your fire; fire slowly, deliberately—above all, fire low, and be always sure of your aim. Close readily in upon the enemy, and when you get within charging distance, rush upon him with the bayonet. Do this and victory will certainly be yours.
—Union General William Rosecrans, Battle Orders, from Headquarters, Department of the Cumberland, near Murfreesboro, Tennessee, December 31, 1862
[RR 6]

Never mind! Brave men must die in battle. We must seek results.
—Union General William Rosecrans, remark after hearing of the death of General J. W. Sill, Stones River, December 31
[RR 6, doc 161]

Bragg's a good dog, but Hold Fast's a better.
—Attributed to Union General William Rosecrans, who called himself "Hold Fast," for countering Confederate General Braxton Bragg at the Battle of Stones River, December 31, 1862 and January 2, 1863
[CWD, 79]

I am sick and tired of this war, and I can see no prospects of having peace for a long time to come. I don't think it ever will be stopped by fighting. The Yankees can't whip us and we can never whip them, and I see no prospect of peace unless the Yankees themselves rebel and throw down their arms, and refuse to fight any longer.
—Confederate soldier, letter, after the Battle of Stones River, January 2, 1863
[CWDD, 307]

❖❖❖

1863

FINAL EMANCIPATION PROCLAMATION

With the Emancipation Proclamation's implementation into law, there was celebration in the North as well as in Southern communities that Union armies had already reclaimed. Jefferson Davis, president of the Confederacy, continued to disparage the character of the Yankees and to argue that the government of the South, not the North, was the true heir of American democracy.

I never in my life felt more certain that I was doing right than I do in signing this paper.

    —President Abraham Lincoln, remarking as he signed the "Final Emancipation Proclamation," January 1, 1863
    [CW-2]

. . . I do order and declare that all persons held as slaves within said designated States, and parts of States, are, and henceforward shall be free; and that the Executive government of the United States, including the military and naval authorities thereof, will recognize and maintain the freedom of said persons.

    —President Abraham Lincoln, "Final Emancipation Proclamation," January 1, 1863
    [GS]

Mark our words! If we succeed, the children of these very men who are now fighting us will rise up to call us blessed. Just as surely as there is a God who governs the world, so surely all the laws of national prosperity follow in the train of equity; and if we

succeed, we shall have delivered the children's children of our misguided brethren from the wages of sin, which is always and everywhere death.
    —Harriet Beecher Stowe, author of *Uncle Tom's Cabin,* in an article in the *Atlantic Monthly,* January 1863
    [WW]

"What shall be done with the slaves if they are freed?" You had better ask, "What shall we do with the slaveholders if the slaves are freed?" The slave has shown himself better fitted to take care of himself than the slaveholder.
    —William W. Brown, author and former slave
    [BM]

I am happy to be welcomed on my return to the capital of the Confederacy—the last hope, as I believe, for the perpetuation of that system of government which our forefathers founded—the asylum of the oppressed, and the home of true representative liberty.
    —Confederate President Jefferson Davis, on the portico of the Confederate White House, Richmond, Virginia, January 5, 1863
    [CW-2]

The people of this Confederacy . . . cannot fail to receive this proclamation as the fullest vindication of their own sagacity in foreseeing the uses to which the dominant party in the United States intended from the beginning to apply their power; nor can they cease to remember with devout thankfulness that it is to their own vigilance in resisting the first stealthy progress of approaching despotism that they owe their escape from consequences now apparent to the most skeptical.
    —Confederate President Jefferson Davis, message to the Senate and House of Representatives of the Confederate States, Richmond, Virginia, January 12, 1863
    [RR 6, 381]

❖❖❖

I want to be a soldier,
And with the soldiers stand,
A knapsack on my shoulder,
And musket in my hand;
And there beside Jeff Davis,
So glorious and so brave,
I'll whip the cussed Yankee
And drive him to his grave.
—Confederate song, "I Want to Be a Soldier"
[CWT: ref: *The War Comes to Richmond Children,* 1885]

I want to be a soldier,
And go to Dixie's Land,
A knapsack on my shoulder,
And a gun in my hand;
Then I will shoot Jeff Davis
And Beauregard I will hang,
And make all Rebels tremble
Throughout our glorious land.
—Union song, "I Want to Be a Soldier." ("We are on one side of the Rappahannock, the enemy on the other. . . . Our boys will sing a Southern song, the Yankees will reply by singing the same tune to Yankee words," wrote Confederate Lieutenant W. J. Kincheloe in a letter to his father, January 12, 1863.)
[CWT]

Carolinians and Georgians! The hour is at hand to prove your devotion to your country's cause. Let all able-bodied men, from the seaboard to the mountains, rush to arms. Be not exacting in the choice of weapons; pikes and scythes will do for exterminating your enemies, spades and shovels for protecting your friends. To arms, fellow citizens! Come share with us our dangers, our brilliant success, or our glorious death.
—Confederate General P. G. T. Beauregard, commander of the defenses of the Carolina and Georgia coasts, proclamation, January 18, 1863
[RR 6]

❖❖❖

Slavery must die, and if the South insists on being buried in the same grave I shall see in it nothing but the retributive hand of God.

—Union Corporal Rufus Kinsley, diary, January 21, 1863
[BY]

The war can be ended only by annihilating that Oligarchy which formed and rules the South and makes the war—by annihilating a state of society.

—Wendell Phillips, abolitionist, newspaper, January 23, 1863
[BCF]

We are like whalers who have been on a long chase. We have at last got the harpoon into the monster, but we must look now how we steer, or with one flop of his tail he will send us all into eternity.

—President Abraham Lincoln, in conversation to a friend, January, 1863
[RWAL: ref: Henry J. Raymond, *The Life, Public Services, and State Papers of Abraham Lincoln*, New York: Darvy and Miller, 1865, 752]

Two years have passed and the rebel flag still haunts our nation's capital. Our armies enter the best rebel territory and the wave closes in behind. The utmost we can claim is that our enemy respects our power to do them physical harm more than they did at first; but as to loving us any more, it were idle even to claim it. . . . I still see no end, or even the beginning of the end.

—Union General William Tecumseh Sherman, letter to his brother, Senator John Sherman of Ohio, late January 1863
[CW-2]

I hold that the Proclamation, good as it is, will be worthless—a miserable mockery—unless the nation shall so far conquer its prejudice as to welcome into the army full-grown black men to help fight the battles of the Republic.

—Frederick Douglass, author and abolitionist, New York City, February 6, 1863
[WW]

———————❖❖❖———————

This winter was a quiet season for the war, as severe cold set in. Even so, battles continued at sea and from coast to coast. Hospitals were full of wounded soldiers.

It was a grand, though fearful sight, to see the guns belching forth, in the darkness of the night, sheets of living flame, the deadly missiles striking the enemy with a force that we could *feel.*

> —Anonymous Confederate officer, on the *Alabama* destroying the Union steamer *Hatteras*, Galveston Harbor, Texas, January 11, 1863
> [Harwell, *The Confederate Reader*]

You believe yourselves very generous and think because you have voted this petty sum [to the Ladies' Aid Society] you are doing all that is required of you. But I have in my hospital a hundred poor soldiers who have done more than any of you. Who of you would contribute a leg, an arm or an eye, instead of what you have done? How many hundred or thousand dollars would you consider an equivalent for either? Don't deceive yourselves gentlemen. The poor soldier who has given an arm, a leg or an eye to his country (and many of them have given much more than one) has given more than you have or can. How much more, then, he who has given his life? No! gentlemen, you must set your standard higher yet or you will not come up to the full measure of liberality in giving.

> —Mary Ann "Mother" Bickerdyke, address to the Milwaukee Chamber of Commerce
> [BV 181]

The soldier's hospital! How many sleepless nights, how many woman's tears, how many long and aching hours and days of suspense, from every one of the Middle, Eastern and Western States have concentrated here!

> —Walt Whitman, poet and correspondent, *New-York Times*, February 26, 1863
> [*New-York Times*, February 26, 1863]

❖❖❖

Bearing the bandages, water and sponge,
Straight and swift to my wounded I go,
Where they lie on the ground after the battle brought in,
Where their priceless blood reddens the grass the ground,
Or to the rows of the hospital tent, or under the roof'd hospital,
To the long rows of cots up and down each side I return,
To each and all one after another I draw near, not one do I miss,
An attendant follows holding a tray, he carries a refuse pail,
Soon to be fill'd with clotted rags and blood, emptied, and
    fill'd again.
—Walt Whitman, "The Wound-Dresser." (Besides working as a
reporter, Whitman also served as a nurse in Union hospitals.)
[CWP]

Our Jimmy has gone for to live in a tent,
They have grafted him into the army;
He finally pucker'd up courage and went,
When they grafted him into the army.
—"Grafted into the Army," song by Henry Clay Work, after
Congress enacted the draft in March 1863
[UR]

The men are ill-dressed, ill-equipped, and ill-provided, a set of
ragamuffins that a man is ashamed to be seen among, even
when he is a prisoner and can't help it. And yet they have beaten
us fairly, beaten us all to pieces, beaten us so easily that we are
objects of contempt even to their commonest private soldiers,
with no shirts to hang out the holes of their pantaloons, and
cartridge-boxes tied around their waists with strands of rope.
—Union officer, after being exchanged from a Confederate prison
camp, spring 1863
[CW-2]

We have met with a sad repulse; I shall not turn it into a great
disaster.
—Union Rear Admiral Samuel Francis Du Pont, on his ships failing
to take Charleston, South Carolina, April 7, 1863. (Du Pont gave up
his command in July.)
[CW-2]

❖❖❖

We have reached the close of the second year of the war, and may point with just pride to the history of our young Confederacy. Alone, unaided, we have met and overthrown the most formidable combination of naval and military armaments that the lust of conquest ever gathered together for the subjugation of a free people.

> —Confederate President Jefferson Davis, proclamation, "To the People of the Confederate States," April 10, 1863
> [CW-2]

As to the reports in newspapers, we must scorn them, else they will ruin us and our country. They are as much enemies to good government as the secesh, and between the two I like the secesh best, because they are a brave, open enemy and not a set of sneaking, croaking scoundrels.

> —Union General William Tecumseh Sherman, letter to his wife, late April 1863. (Sherman was particularly hostile to journalists, having felt persecuted and misrepresented by them earlier in the war.)
> [CW-2]

Shoot up everything blue and keep up the scare.

> —Confederate General Nathan Bedford Forrest, during a moonlight attack on Union Colonel Abel Streight's men at Crooked Creek, Alabama, April 30, 1863
> [CW-2]

My principle is to kill a Yankee wherever I find him. If they don't like that, let them stay at home.

> —Confederate scout William D. Farley
> [CW-2]

We have all come to the conclusion that they [the American revolutionaries of 1776] had a right to be independent, and it was best they should be. Nor can we escape from the inference that the Federals will one day come to the same conclusion with regard to the Southern States.

> —*London Times*, May 2, 1863
> [CW-2]

❖❖❖

CHANCELLORSVILLE CAMPAIGN AND THE DEATH OF STONEWALL JACKSON

Major General Joseph Hooker became commander of the Army of the Potomac in late January, after his predecessor, Ambrose Burnside, requested either Hooker's dismissal or the acceptance of his own resignation. Hooker had not been particularly loyal to Lincoln, but he was a big talker and had a reputation as a fighter, and Lincoln chose him to carry out the Union advance in Virginia. The Army of the Potomac began making its way across the Rappahannock River, near the Wilderness area, on April 28. After the first day's battle on May 1, though Richmond lay vulnerable beyond Lee's necessarily defensive-minded and quite smaller Army of Northern Virginia, Hooker gave up the attack and went into a defensive mode. On the night of May 1, Confederate Generals Lee and Jackson came up with a daring plan to attack Hooker's stalled army near a clearing in the Wilderness called Chancellorsville. In the wildly successful rout that followed on May 2, Jackson was shot in the dim light by his own men, who mistook him for a Union officer as he returned to his lines. The loss of Jackson perhaps meant more than the victory to the Confederacy.

Beware of rashness, but with energy and sleepless vigilance go forward and give us victories.
—President Abraham Lincoln, letter to Major General Joseph Hooker, giving Hooker command of the Army of the Potomac, January 26, 1863
[CWD, 410]

The Union boys are moving on the left and on the right,
The bugle call is sounding, our shelters we must strike;
Joe Hooker is our leader, he takes his whiskey strong,
So our knapsacks we will sling, and go marching along.
—Song, by Union Major General Joseph Hooker's veterans, on the Chancellorsville campaign
[CW-2]

❖❖❖

I have no confidence in General Hooker. Burnside was stuck in the mud, and he will be stuck worse.

—Union Lieutenant Gilbert S. Lawrence, who was dismissed from the army for saying this in front of other officers and civilians as well as declaring, "Nobody but McClellan can command this army," March 3, 1863
[RR 6]

My plans are perfect, and when I start to carry them out, may God have mercy on Bobby Lee, for I shall have none.

—Union Major General Joseph Hooker, commander of the Army of the Potomac, in conversation, April 12, 1863
[CW-2]

If you cannot cut off from his column large slices, the general desires that you will not fail to take small ones. Let your watchword be fight, fight, fight, bearing in mind that time is as valuable to the general as rebel carcasses.

—Union Major General Joseph Hooker's adjutant, delivering a message from Hooker, to Cavalry Corps Commander General George Stoneman, April 12, 1863. (Stoneman's cavalry was not able to do this ambitious and timely work, as the flooding of the Rappahannock delayed his raids by two weeks.)
[CW-2]

It is with heartfelt satisfaction that the commanding general announces to the army that the operations of the last three days have determined that our enemy must either ingloriously fly, or come out from behind his defenses and give us battle on our own ground, where certain destruction awaits him.

—Union Major General Joseph Hooker, General Orders No. 47, the Army of the Potomac, at Chancellorsville, camp near Falmouth, Virginia, April 30, 1863
[RR 6]

Just as "yon level sun" was sending the shadows of the forest trees across the meadow, there was a roar and crash of arms almost in the rear and seeming to come, as it really did, from the very place that the division had occupied but a few hours before.

———— ❖❖❖ ————

It was the first blast of the cyclone that swept the Eleventh Corps from its position on the right of the Union line like chaff from a threshing floor.
—Union Captain Asa W. Bartlett, on Stonewall Jackson's devastating flanking attack, May 2, 1863
[NHV, 73]

On the one hand was a solid column of infantry retreating in double quick from the face of the enemy; on the other was a dense mass of being who had lost their reasoning faculties, and were flying from a thousand fancied dangers.
—Thomas Cook, *New York Herald,* on Stonewall Jackson's attack and the resulting Union panic on May 2, 1863
[SS]

I was not hurt by a shell, and I was not drunk. For once I lost confidence in Joe Hooker, and that is all there is to it.
—Union Major General Joseph Hooker, after the huge loss at the Battle of Chancellorsville. This remark was attributed to him "some weeks later," in private conversation
[CW-2]

What an infinite blessing . . . blessing . . . blessing.
—Confederate General Stonewall Jackson, under chloroform, before Dr. Hunter McGuire amputated his left arm, the early morning after the night he was shot by his own men as he returned to his lines in the twilight, May 2, 1863
[TJJ]

Thank God it is no worse; God be praised that he is still alive. Any victory is a dear one that deprives us of the services of Jackson, even for a short time.
—Confederate General Robert E. Lee, to the messenger who delivered the news of Jackson's wounding, after the battle of Chancellorsville, May 3, 1863
[RR 6]

❖❖❖

. . . tell him to make haste and get well and come back to me as soon as he can. He has lost his left arm; but I have lost my right arm.
　　—Confederate General Robert E. Lee, to Chaplain Beverly Tucker Lacy, about Stonewall Jackson's amputation
　　[BG, 263]

I am wounded but not depressed. I believe it was God's will, and I can wait until He makes his object known to me.
　　—Confederate General Stonewall Jackson, May 3, 1863, having awakened after his amputation. Pneumonia soon set in.
　　[CW-2]

Surely General Jackson will recover. God will not take him from us, now that we need him so much.
　　—Confederate General Robert E. Lee, to Chaplain Lacy, upon hearing that Stonewall Jackson was dying, May 9, 1863
　　[TJJ]

Let us cross over the river, and rest under the shade of the trees.
　　—Stonewall Jackson's dying words, near Fredericksburg, Virginia, May 10, 1863
　　[TJJ]

> Dead is the Man whose Cause is dead,
> Vainly he died and set his seal—
> Stonewall!
> Earnest in error, as we feel;
> True to the thing he deemed was due,
> True as John Brown or steel.

　　—Herman Melville, from the poem "Stonewall Jackson"
　　[CWP]

I think there is a popular delusion about the amount of praying [Stonewall] Jackson did. He certainly preferred a fight on Sunday to a sermon. Failing to manage a fight, he loved next best a long Presbyterian sermon, Calvinistic to the core.
　　—Confederate General Alexander R. Lawton, quoted by Mary Boykin Chesnut in her diary, Richmond, Virginia, December 5, 1863. (Lawton fought under Jackson in the Shenandoah Valley

❖❖❖

campaign. He also remarked: "But be ye sure, it was bitter hard work to keep up with Stonewall Jackson, as all know who ever served with him. He gave his orders rapidly and distinctly, and rode away without allowing answer or remonstrance. When you failed, you were apt to be put under arrest. When you succeeded, he only said 'good.'")
[CWT: ref: Mary Boykin Chesnut, *A Diary from Dixie*, 1949]

✿

VICKSBURG CAMPAIGN

Vicksburg, Mississippi, on the bluffs of the Mississippi River, was a target of the Union from the spring of 1862, when Admiral Farragut demanded its surrender, until its capitulation on July 4, 1863. Major General Ulysses S. Grant, the head of the Army of the Tennessee from the fall of 1862, tried many unsuccessful approaches before hitting on a combined operation with Admiral Porter's ships and various diversionary raids that allowed Grant's forces to land on the eastern side of the Mississippi below Vicksburg on April 30, 1863.

The work of reducing Vicksburg will take time and men, but can be accomplished.
—Major General Ulysses S. Grant, Memphis, Tennessee, letter to General Henry Halleck, Washington, D.C., January 20, 1863
[OR 1, Vol 24, Pt. 1, 9]

One thing is certain; two generals cannot command this army, issuing independent and direct orders to subordinate officers, and the public service be promoted.
—Union General John McClernand, letter to Major General Ulysses S. Grant, January 30, 1863. (Grant later expressed this idea with more punch: "Two commanders on the same field are always one too many." Grant had the overall command, however, and forced McClernand to bow out and become a supporting player. McClernand was a politician from Illinois who had received his military appointment for political considerations.)
[USG]

❖❖❖

. . . Grant, entrusted with our greatest army, is a jackass in the original package. He is a poor drunken imbecile. He is a poor stick sober, and he is most of the time more than half drunk, and much of the time idiotically drunk. . . . Grant will fail miserably, hopelessly, eternally.

> —Marat Halstead, editor of the *Cincinnati Commercial*, letter to Secretary of the Treasury Salmon P. Chase, March 12, 1863
> [CW-2]

The great object on your line now is the opening of the Mississippi River, and everything else must tend to that purpose. The eyes and hopes of the whole country are now directed to your army. In my opinion, the opening of the Mississippi River will be to us of more advantage than the capture of forty Richmonds.

> —Union General in Chief Henry Halleck to Major General Ulysses S. Grant, commander of the Department of the Tennessee, about the Vicksburg campaign, March 20, 1863
> [CW-2]

The hills are so honey-combed with caves that the streets look like avenues in a cemetery.

> —"A Union lady," in Vicksburg during the siege, March 20, 1863
> [BG, 663]

All the campaigns, labors, hardships, and exposures, from the month of December previous to this time, that had been made and endured, were for the accomplishment of this one object.

> —Union Major General Ulysses S. Grant, on the landing of his first troops across the Mississippi, below Vicksburg, April 30, 1863
> [CWDD, 343]

The enemy is badly beaten, greatly demoralized, and exhausted of ammunition. The road to Vicksburg is open. All we want now are men, ammunition, and hard bread. We can subsist our horses on the country, and obtain considerable supplies for our troops.

> —Union Major General Ulysses S. Grant, Grand Gulf, Mississippi, letter to General William Tecumseh Sherman, Vicksburg, May 3, 1863
> [CW-2]

❖❖❖

Tell General Grant that my division cannot be whipped by all
the rebels this side of hell. We are going ahead, and won't stop
till we get orders.
  —General John Logan, to an officer sent "to inquire how the contest was going in his front," at Champion's Hill, May 16, 1863
  [RR VII]

There they lay, the blue and the gray intermingled; the same
rich, young American blood flowing out in little rivulets of crim-
son; each thinking he was in the right.
  —Union soldier, after the battle of Champion's Hill, Mississippi,
  during the Vicksburg campaign, May 16, 1863. (A third of Union
  General Alvin Hovey's forces were killed, wounded, or captured.
  Both sides took and lost the hill several times before the
  Confederates retreated.)
  [CW-2]

While a battle is raging one can see his enemy mowed down by the
thousand, or the ten thousand, with great composure, but after the
battle these scenes are distressing, and one is naturally disposed to
do as much to alleviate the suffering of an enemy as a friend.
  —Union Major General Ulysses S. Grant, reflecting on the battle of
  Champion's Hill
  [USG]

Until this moment I never thought your expedition a success. I
never could see the end clearly until now. But this is a campaign.
This is a success if we never take the town.
  —Union General William Tecumseh Sherman, in conversation with
  Major General Ulysses S. Grant, near Vicksburg, May 17, 1863
  [USG]

Two days having elapsed since your dead and wounded have been
lying in our front, and as yet no disposition on your part of a desire
to remove them being exhibited, in the name of humanity I have
the honor to propose a cessation of hostilities for two hours and a
half, that you may be enabled to remove your dead and dying.
  —Confederate Major General John Pemberton, letter to Union
  Major General Ulysses S. Grant, after a failed assault on Vicksburg,
  May 25, 1863
  [RR 7]

❖❖❖

I will endeavor to hold out as long as we have anything to eat.
—Confederate Major General John Pemberton, letter to General
Joseph Johnston, from Vicksburg, May 25, 1863
[RR 7]

Twenty-four hours of each day these preachers of the Union made their touching remarks to the town. All night long their deadly hail of iron dropped through the roofs and tore up the deserted and denuded streets.
—Citizen of Vicksburg, on the Union bombardment, June 8, 1863
[CWDD, 363]

All that we can attempt to do is to save you and your garrison.
—Confederate General Joseph Johnston, letter to Major General
John Pemberton, June 14, 1863
[RR 7]

I consider saving Vicksburg hopeless.
—Confederate General Joseph Johnston, letter to Secretary of War
James Seddon, June 15, 1863
[O.R. 1, Vol 24, Pt. 1, 228]

On every ground I have great deference to your superior knowledge of the position, your judgment and military genius, but I feel it right to share, if need be to take, the responsibility, and leave you free to follow the most desperate course the occasion may demand. Rely upon it, the eyes and hopes of the whole Confederacy are upon you with the full confidence that you will act, and with the sentiment that it were better to fail nobly daring than, through prudence even, to be in active. . . . I rely on you for all possible efforts to save Vicksburg.
—Confederate Secretary of War James Seddon, letter to General
Joseph Johnston, June 21, 1863. (Johnston later wrote: "I did not
indulge in the sentiment that it was better for me to waste the lives
and blood of brave soldiers 'than, through prudence even,' to spare
them.")
[O.R. 1, Vol 24, Pt. 1, 228]

If you can't feed us, you had better surrender us, horrible as the idea is, than suffer this noble army to disgrace themselves by

❖❖❖

desertion. I tell you plainly men are not going to lie here and perish, if they do love their country dearly. Self-preservation is the first law of nature, and hunger will compel a man to do almost anything.
—"Many Soldiers," letter to Confederate Major General John Pemberton, within besieged Vicksburg, June 28, 1863
[O.R. *Navy*, 1, Vol 25, 118]

Unless the siege of Vicksburg is raised, or supplies are thrown in, it will become necessary very shortly to evacuate the place. I see no prospect of the former, and there are many great, if not insuperable obstacles in the way of the latter.
—Confederate Major General John Pemberton, letter to Generals Carter Stevenson, John Forney, Martin Luther Smith, and John Bowen, July 1, 1863
[RR 7]

The useless effusion of blood you propose stopping by this course can be ended at any time you may choose, by an unconditional surrender of the city and garrison.
—Union Major General Ulysses S. Grant, reply to Confederate Major General John Pemberton's proposal that they call an armistice and negotiate "terms for the capitulation of Vicksburg," July 3, 1863
[RR 7]

Good Heavens! Are these the long-boasted fortifications of Vicksburg? It was the rebels, and not their works, that kept us out of the city.
—Union General James McPherson, after Confederate Major General John Pemberton surrendered to General Grant, July 4, 1863
[Harwell, *Confederate Reader*]

See here, Mister; you man on the little white horse! Danged if you ain't the hardest feller to hit I ever saw. I've shot at you more'n a hundred times.
—Union soldier, calling out to chief engineer and Confederate Major Samuel Lockett, after Vicksburg had been taken, July 4, 1863
[CW-2]

❖❖❖

This is a day of jubilee, a day of rejoicing to the faithful. . . .
Already are my orders out to give one big huzza and sling the
knapsack for new fields.

> —Union General William Tecumseh Sherman, letter to Major
> General Ulysses S. Grant, after hearing that Vicksburg had been
> taken, July 4, 1863
> [CW-2]

. . . even should Lee's army be destroyed and every town in the
South burned, the rebellion would be unsubdued. There are a
hundred thousand men in the South who feel as I do, that they
would rather an earthquake should swallow the whole country
than yield to our oppressors—men who will retire to the mountains and live on acorns, and crawl on their bellies to shoot an
invader wherever they can see one.

> —Confederate Lieutenant Colonel Alston, writing in his journal on
> the news that Vicksburg had fallen, Lexington, Kentucky, July 8,
> 1863
> [RR 7 , 360]

The nailhead that held the South's two halves together.

> —Confederate President Jefferson Davis, on Vicksburg, Mississippi,
> the Confederacy's last anchor on the Mississippi River
> [CW-2]

If I knew what brand of whiskey he drinks I would send a bar-
rel or so to some other generals.

> —Attributed to President Lincoln about Union Major General
> Ulysses S. Grant during Grant's Vicksburg Campaign. Asked
> about it, Lincoln told Secretary of the Treasury Salmon P. Chase
> that he *wished* he had said it. (Another attributed version: ". . . if
> those accusing General Grant of getting drunk will tell me where
> he gets his whiskey, I will get a lot of it and sent it around to some
> of the other generals, who are badly in need of something of
> the kind.")
> [RWAL]

❖❖❖

GETTYSBURG CAMPAIGN

While Grant was taking Vicksburg, the most famous battle of the war was occurring the first three days of July near the town of Gettysburg in southeastern Pennsylvania. Robert E. Lee did not expect his Army of Northern Virginia to conquer the North but to win a dramatic victory on Union ground that would convince the North that the war would not be worthwhile to continue, and, perhaps, after all, gain recognition for the Confederacy by Great Britain. The Confederacy would thereby win its independence. There was also hope that the invasion of Pennsylvania would draw some of the overwhelming number of Union forces from Vicksburg and Chattanooga, thus allowing the Confederate forces in the south and west to have a better chance of resisting. Lincoln lost confidence in Major General Joseph Hooker's ability to take on Lee, so on June 27 replaced Hooker as commander of the Army of the Potomac with Major General George Meade. After the Union victory on July 3, Lincoln became frustrated with Meade for not pursuing and attempting to destroy Lee's army.

. . . our Army would be invincible if it could be properly organized and officered. There never were such men in an Army before. They will go anywhere and do anything if properly led. But there is the difficulty—proper commanders—where can they be obtained?

—Confederate General Robert E. Lee, reply to General John B. Hood, on Hood's plans for a campaign, May 21, 1863
[LL-1, xvii]

If I could take one wing and Lee the other, I think we could between us wrest a victory from those people.

—Confederate President Jefferson Davis, remark to his wife, "one hot June night," 1863. (Davis served in the Mexican War, and was secretary of war of the United States in 1853. Union General Ulysses S. Grant, however, did not highly rate Davis's military acumen, and, many years later, remarked in his *Memoirs:* "On several occasions during the war [Davis] came to the relief of the Union army by means of his superior military genius.")
[CW-2]

❖❖❖

I think Lee's Army, and not Richmond, is your true objective point. . . . Fight him when opportunity offers. If he stays where he is, fret him, and fret him.

—President Abraham Lincoln, message to Major General Joseph Hooker, June 10, 1863. (Lee's Army of Northern Virginia had begun its invasion campaign, and Hooker, feeling helpless to stop the invasion, saw on the other hand an opportunity to take Richmond.)
[CWDD, 364]

If the head of Lee's army is at Martinsburg and the tail of it on the plank road between Fredericksburg and Chancellorsville, the animal must be very slim somewhere. Could you not break it now?

—President Abraham Lincoln, letter to Major General Joseph Hooker, June 16, 1863. (On June 15, Lee's army began crossing the Potomac into Maryland.)
[BG, 594]

I can fight so much harder since I have got a grudge against them. It is my honest wish that my rifle may draw tears from many a northern mother and sighs from many a father before this thing is over.

—Confederate soldier James Yates, letter to his mother in Mississippi (whose home had been raided by Union soldiers), on his way to Gettysburg, June 17, 1863
[JR]

My only desire is that they will let me go home and eat my bread in peace.

—Confederate General Robert E. Lee, to a Union-sympathizing woman of Chambersburg, Pennsylvania, June 27, 1863
[CW-2]

It must be remembered that we make war only upon armed men, and that we cannot take vengeance for the wrongs our people have suffered without lowering ourselves in the eyes of all whose abhorrence has been excited by the atrocities of our enemy, and offending against Him to whom vengeance belongeth, and without whose favor and support our efforts must all prove in vain.

—Confederate General Robert E. Lee, address to his soldiers on the advance into Pennsylvania, near Chambersburg, June 27, 1863
[RR 7, Doc, 323]

❖❖❖

I felt when I first came here, that I would like to revenge myself upon these people for the desolation they have brought upon our own beautiful home; that home where we could have lived so happy, and that we loved so much, from which their vandalism has driven you and my helpless little ones. But though I had such severe wrongs and grievances to redress, yet when I got among these people I could not find it in my heart to molest them.

—Confederate Officer William Christian, letter to his wife, from near Greenwood, Pennsylvania, June 28, 1863
[RR 7, Doc, 325]

Can you tell me where General Stuart is? Where on earth is my cavalry?

—Confederate General Robert E. Lee, before Chambersburg, Pennsylvania, while his cavalry General J. E. B. Stuart's raiding force was seventy miles away, June 28, 1863
[CW-2]

General Meade will commit no blunder on my front, and if I make one he will make haste to take advantage of it.

—Confederate General Robert E. Lee, remarking on General George Meade taking over the Union Army of the Potomac, June 29, 1863. (Lee knew Meade from their U.S. Army days.)
[CW-2]

The enemy are advancing in strong force, and . . . . I fear they will get to the heights beyond the town before I can. I will fight him inch by inch, and if driven into the town, I will barricade the streets and hold him back as long as possible.

—Union General John Fulton Reynolds, near Gettysburg, July 1, 1863
[http://www.civilweek.com/1863/jul0163Sup.htm]

Forward, forward, men! Drive those fellows out of that! Forward! For God's sake, forward!

—Union General John Fulton Reynolds, last words, before he was shot dead by a sniper at Gettysburg, July 1, 1863
[CW-2]

———❖❖❖———

They are there in position, and I am going to whip them or they are going to whip me.
—Confederate General Robert E. Lee, to General James Longstreet, about the Union force near Cemetery Hill, Gettysburg, July 1, 1863. (Longstreet replied, "If he is there, it will be because he is anxious that we should attack him; a good reason, in my judgment, for not doing so.")
[CW-2]

Longstreet is a very good fighter when he gets in position and gets everything ready, but he is so slow.
—Confederate General Robert E. Lee, remark to General Jubal Early on General James Longstreet, as Lee tried to determine the next day's strategy at Gettysburg, July 1, 1863
[CW-2]

General Stuart, where have you been? I have not heard a word from you in days, and you the eyes and ears of my army.
—Confederate General Robert E. Lee to cavalry General J. E. B. Stuart, July 2, 1863
[CW-2]

Compliments, hell! Who wants compliments in such a damned place as this? Go back and ask General Law if he expects me to hold the world in check with the 5th regiment!
—Confederate Major J. C. Rogers, who led the Texas regiments in the attack on the Round Tops at Gettysburg after several field officers above him were killed or wounded, to a courier from General Evander Law, July 2, 1863.
[CW-2]

The general is a little nervous this morning. He wishes me to attack. I do not wish to do so without Pickett. I never like to go into battle with one boot off.
—Confederate General James Longstreet, in conversation with General J. B. Hood, about General Robert E. Lee, July 3, 1863
[CW-2]

❖❖❖

I do not want to make this charge. I do not see how it can succeed. I would not make it now but that General Lee has ordered
it and expects it.

>—Confederate General James Longstreet, preparing to command
>General George Pickett's charge, July 3, 1863
>[CW-2]

I could see the desperate and hopeless nature of the charge and
the hopeless slaughter it would cause. . . . That day at
Gettysburg was one of the saddest of my life.

>—Confederate General James Longstreet, reflecting on Pickett's
>charge, Gettysburg, July 3, 1863
>[BCF]

The air was all murderous iron.

>—Union soldier under General John Gibbon, on the artillery fire
>that preceded Confederate General George Pickett's charge, July 3,
>1863
>[CW-2]

Men fire into each other's faces, not five feet apart. There are
bayonet-thrusts, sabre-strokes, pistol-shots; . . . men going down
on their hands and knees, spinning round like tops, throwing out
their arms, gulping up blood, falling; legless, armless, headless.
There are ghastly heaps of dead men . . .

>—An "eyewitness," of Pickett's charge, July 3, 1863
>[CWDD, 377]

It's all my fault. It is I who have lost this fight, and you must help
me out of it the best way you can. All good men must rally.

>—Confederate General Robert E. Lee, to his soldiers, after
>Pickett's charge, Gettysburg, July 3, 1863
>[BG, 637]

Come, General Pickett. This has been my fight, and upon my
shoulders rests the blame. The men and officers of your command have written the name of Virginia as high today as it has

❖❖❖

ever been written before. . . . Your men have done all that men can do. The fault is entirely my own.

—Confederate General Robert E. Lee to the disconsolate Pickett, after the catastrophic charge, July 3, 1863
[CW-2]

Well, it is all over now. The awful rain of shot and shell was a sob—a gasp. I can still hear them cheering as I gave the order, "Forward!" the thrill of their joyous voices as they called out, "We'll follow you, Marse George, we'll follow you!" Oh, how faithfully they followed me on—on—to their death, and I led them on—on—on—Oh, God!

—Confederate General George Pickett, letter to his fiancée, on the charge named after him at Gettysburg, July 3, 1863
[WW]

Each man felt, as he tightened his saber belt, that he was summoned to a ride to death.

—Union cavalry Captain H. C. Parsons, reflecting on the suicidal charge led by General Elon Farnsworth (on orders from General Hugh Kilpatrick that Farnsworth hotly protested), at Gettysburg, July 3, 1863
[CW-2]

We must now return to Virginia.

—Confederate General Robert E. Lee, after deciding to withdraw the army from Gettysburg, July 3, 1863
[CW-2]

If I had had Stonewall Jackson with me, so far as man can see, I should have won the battle of Gettysburg.

—Confederate General Robert E. Lee, in reflection, "to a friend"
[CW-2]

Ah, General Meade, you're in very great danger of being President of the United States.

—Anonymous journalist "W," to General George Meade, moments after the tide of battle turned to the Union at Gettysburg. (Meade, however, having been born in Spain, to American parents, was not eligible to run for the presidency.)
[RR 7]

❖❖❖

I was glad to do a little something for them. . . . Utterly as I detest a living active rebel, as soon as he becomes wounded and a prisoner, I don't perceive any differences in my feelings toward him and towards one of our wounded heroes.

—Union Captain William Wheeler, about the battlefields of Gettysburg, letter home, July 1863
[BY: ref: *In Memoriam: Letters of William Wheeler of the Class of 1855*, *Y.C.*, 414]

The rebels are hunted out of the North, their best army is routed, and the charm of Robert Lee's invincibility is broken. The Army of the Potomac has at last found a general that can handle it, and has stood nobly up to its terrible work in spite of its long disheartening list of hard-fought failures.

—George Templeton Strong, of New York, diary, after news of Gettysburg reached New York City, July 6, 1863
[GTS, 330]

Ah! what a terrible responsibility rests upon those who inaugurated this unholy war.

—Citizen of Clarksville, Virginia, hearing of the disaster to the soldiers from its town at Gettysburg
[CW-2]

"Stop! oh! For God's sake, stop just for one minute, take me out and leave me to die on the roadside." No heed could be given to any of their appeals. . . . During this one night I realized more of the horrors of war than I had in all the two preceding years.

—Confederate Brigadier General John D. Imboden, on the suffering of the wounded, as they were raced away in bare wagons, starving and dying, from Gettysburg, July 4, 1863
[CW-2]

From the time I took command till today, I . . . have not had a regular night's rest, and many nights not a wink of sleep, and for several days did not even wash my face and hands, no regular food, and all the time in a state of mental anxiety. Indeed, I think I have lived as much in this time as in the last thirty years.

—Union General George Meade, letter to his wife, July 7, 1863
[CW-2]

❖❖❖

DEAR MOTHER: I may not again see you but do not fear for your tired soldier boy. Death has no fears for me. My hope is still firm in Jesus. Meet me and Father in heaven with all my dear friends. I have no special message to send you, but bid you all a happy farewell.

> —Union sergeant Charles Ward, wounded at Gettysburg, letter to his mother, July 7, 1863. Ward died July 9.
> [BY]

I felt a joyous exaltation, a perfect indifference to circumstances through the whole of that three days fight, and have seldom enjoyed three days more in my life.

> —Union artilleryman John P. Sheahan, letter to his father, after Gettysburg, July 10, 1863
> [BY]

They will be ready to fight a magnificent battle when there is no enemy there to fight.

> —President Abraham Lincoln, remark after reading General George Meade's telegraph message that the Army of the Potomac would be ready to attack the next day, July 12, 1863
> [RWAL: ref: Albert Chandler, "Lincoln and the Telegrapher," *American Heritage,* 12 (April 1961)]

You are strong enough to attack and defeat the enemy before he can effect a crossing. Act upon your own judgment and make your generals execute your orders. Call no council of war. It is proverbial that councils of war never fight. . . . Do not let the enemy escape.

> —Union Major General Henry Halleck, letter to General George Meade, July 13, 1863. Meade finally started after Lee's Army of Northern Virginia on July 14, but almost all of Lee's soldiers had already got across the Potomac into Virginia.
> [CW-2]

We had them in our grasp. We had only to stretch forth our hands and they were ours. And nothing I could say or do could make the army move.

> —President Abraham Lincoln, conversation to John Hay about General George Meade, July 14, 1863
> [Hay, J.]

❖❖❖

The men are in good health and spirits, but want shoes and clothing badly. . . . As soon as these necessary articles are obtained, we shall be prepared to resume operations.
　—Confederate General Robert E. Lee, letter to President Jefferson Davis, from Bunker Hill, Virginia, July 16, 1863

My shoes are gone; my clothes are almost gone. I'm weary, I'm sick, I'm hungry. My family have been killed or scattered, and may be now wandering helpless and unprotected in a strange country. And I have suffered all this for my country. I love my country. I would die—yes, I would die willingly because I love my country. But if this war is ever over, I'll be damned if I ever love another country.
　—Confederate soldier in Longstreet's army
　[ME, 104]

Our army held the war in the hollow of their hand, and they would not close it. We had gone through all the labor of tilling and planting an enormous crop, and when it was ripe we did not harvest it.
　—President Abraham Lincoln, in conversation with his assistant private secretary, John Hay, about Gettysburg, July 19, 1863
　[LCW]

What can I do with such generals as we now have? Who among them is any better than Meade? To sweep away the whole of them from the chief command and substitute a new man would cause a shock and be likely to lead to combinations and troubles greater than we have now.
　—President Abraham Lincoln
　[NCR, 299]

It is meet that when trials and reverses befall us we should seek to take home to our hearts and consciences the lessons which they teach, and profit by the self-examination for which they prepare us. Had not our successes on land and sea made us self-confident and forgetful of our reliance on Him; had not love of lucre eaten like a gangrene into the very heart of the land, converting too many among us into worshippers of gain and ren-

❖❖❖

dering them unmindful of their duty to their country, to their fellow-men, and to their God—who then will presume to complain that we have been chastened or to despair of our just cause and the protection of our heavenly Father?
　　—Confederate President Jefferson Davis, proclamation, July 25, 1863
　　[RR 7, 370]

Yesterday we rode on the pinnacle of success; today absolute ruin seems to be our portion. The Confederacy totters to its destruction.
　　—Confederate Chief of Ordnance Josiah Gorgas, diary, on the news from Gettysburg and Vicksburg, July 28, 1863
　　[CW-2; BCF]

. . . no one is more aware than myself of my inability for the duties of my position. I cannot even accomplish what I myself desire. How can I fulfill the expectations of others?
　　—Confederate General Robert E. Lee, letter to Jefferson Davis, requesting that Davis replace him with another commander of the Army of Northern Virginia, August 8, 1863. (Davis replied on August 11: "To ask me to substitute you by some one in my judgment more fit to command, or who would possess more of the confidence of the army, or of the reflecting men of the country, is to demand an impossibility." Dissuaded from resigning, Lee continued as commander until the surrender of his army in April 1865.)
　　[BG, 640]

Do you know, General, what your attitude toward Lee for a week after the battle reminded me of? . . . I'll be hanged if I could think of anything else than an old woman trying to shoo her geese across a creek.
　　—President Abraham Lincoln in conversation with General George Meade about Meade's lack of pursuit of Lee's Army of Northern Viriginia, which escaped across the Potomac, after Gettysburg in July, October 23, 1863
　　[CW-2]

❖❖❖

The victory at Vicksburg meant that the Union had control of the Mississippi River and could resume full use of it, and that the South was divided. And while General Robert E. Lee was despondent over the loss at Gettysburg, Confederate President Jefferson Davis continued his optimistic pronouncements.

> The Union forever, Hurrah! boys, Hurrah!
> Down with the traitor, up with the stars;
> While we rally round the flag, boys, rally once again,
> Shouting the battle cry of Freedom.

—"The Battle-Cry of Freedom," song by George Frederick Root
[AHD]

If it was any other day I might consider the demand, but the Fourth of July was a bad day to talk about surrender, and I must therefore decline.

—Union Colonel Hanson, remark to Confederate General John Morgan's messenger, demanding unconditional surrender, July 4, 1863, New Market, Kentucky. (Hanson surrendered the town the next day.)
[RR 7, Doc, 358]

You do not appear to observe the fact that this noble army has driven the rebels from Middle Tennessee. . . . I beg in behalf of this army that the War Department may not overlook so great an event because it is not written in letters of blood.

—Union General William Rosecrans, reply to Secretary of War Edwin Stanton's message pointing out the victories at Vicksburg and Gettysburg, July 7, 1863
[BCF]

> John Morgan's foot is on the shore,
> Kentucky! O Kentucky!
> His hand is on thy stable-door,
> Kentucky! O Kentucky!

❖❖❖

You'll see your good gray mare no more,
He'll ride her till her back is sore,
And leave her at some stranger's door,
Kentucky! O Kentucky!

—"Kentucky! O Kentucky!" by Anonymous, on the Confederate raider John Morgan
[RR 8, Poetry, 58]

For the first time I felt sorry for the brave fellows. If their cause is not just, they have been true to it and it must be like death itself for a brave fighter to lay his arms down before his enemy.

—Union soldier Lawrence Van Alstyne, on the captured Confederate soldiers at Port Hudson, Louisiana, July 9, 1863
[BY]

✿

"COLORED" SOLDIERS

It had taken some time for the Union army to enlist African-Americans and former slaves as soldiers, but once it did, the "Colored" brigades served well and provided the Union with a resource lost to the Confederacy, which did not allow the recruitment of nonwhite soldiers into its army until the last weeks of the war. The U.S. Government authorized the employment of African-American troops in the Department of the South on August 25, 1862, and the first black regiment was mustered in New Orleans in September 1862. The First South Carolina Volunteer Infantry was formed under Colonel T. H. Higginson, a Concord, Massachusetts, abolitionist. Higginson's extraordinary book, Army Life in a Black Regiment *(1870), describes his regiment's adventures and battles in the South. Some Confederate forces reacted to the Union's use of such soldiers with hostility and ire, executing captured African-American soldiers and their officers. (See, in particular, the section "The Fort Pillow Massacre" in 1864.)*

Should it ever be its good fortune to get into action, I have no fear but it will win its way to the confidence of those who are willing to recognize courage and manhood, and vindicate the

◆◆◆

wise policy of the Administration, in putting these men into the field and giving them a chance to strike a blow for the country and their own liberty.
—General R. Saxton, letter to Secretary of War Edwin Stanton, on the completion of the organization of the 1st Regiment of Colored South Carolina Volunteers, Beaufort, South Carolina, January 25, 1863
[RR 6]

> To God be the glory! They call us! we come!
> How welcome the watchword, the hurry, the hum!
> Our hearts are aflame as our good swords we bare—
> "For Freedom! for Freedom!" soft echoes the air;
> The bugle rings cheerly; our banners float high;
> O comrades, all forward! we'll triumph or die!

—"Response of the Colored Soldiers," Edna Dean Proctor, 1863, on the enlistment of African-Americans
[RR 8, Poetry, 2]

The colored population is the great available and yet unavailed of, force for restoring the Union. The bare sight of fifty thousand armed and drilled black soldiers on the banks of the Mississippi would end the rebellion at once.
—President Abraham Lincoln, letter to Governor Andrew Johnson of Tennessee, March 26, 1863
[CWDD, 332]

Ise eighty-eight year old, mas'r. . . . Too ole for come? Mas'r joking. Neber too ole for leave de land o' bondage.
—Anonymous slave, freed in South Carolina by Union Colonel Thomas Wentworth Higginson's First South Carolina "Colored" Volunteers, July 10, 1863
[ALBR]

The question that negroes will fight is settled; besides, they make better soldiers in every respect than any troops I have ever had under my command.
—Union General James Blunt, letter to a friend on the July 17 battle at Honey Springs, Oklahoma, July 25, 1863
[RR 7, Doc, 381]

❖❖❖

You say you will not fight to free negroes. Some of them seem willing to fight for you; but, no matter. Fight you, then, exclusively to save the Union. I issued the proclamation on purpose to aid you in saving the Union.
—President Abraham Lincoln, reply declining James C. Conkling's invitation to a Union meeting in Illinois, where there would be objections voiced over the emancipation of the slaves, August 16, 1863
[BCF, 687]

Previous to the formation of colored troops I had a strong inclination to prepare myself for the ministry; but when the country called for *all persons,* I could best serve my God by serving my country and my oppressed brothers. The sequel is short—I enlisted for the war.
—Union Sergeant William H. Carney, 54th (Colored) Regiment of the Massachusetts Volunteers, letter from Morris Island, South Carolina, October 13, 1863
[RR 8, Poetry 16]

Of all the whole creation in the east or in the west,
The glorious Yankee nation is the greatest and the best.
Come along! Come along! don't be alarmed,
Uncle Sam is rich enough to give you all a farm.
—Song, by an anonymous private, 54th (Colored) Regiment of the Massachusetts Volunteers
[CWT: ref: William Wells Brown, *The Negro in the American Rebellion: His Heroism and His Fidelity,* 1880]

We can do this more effectually than the North can now do, for we can give the Negro not only his own freedom, but that of his wife and child, and can secure it to him in his old home.
—Confederate General Patrick Cleburne, proposal to emancipate and enlist the slaves, January 1864. (The proposal outraged many Southerners, but in 1865, Confederate President Jefferson Davis approved a law allowing the enlistment of slaves as soldiers.)
[CW-3]

Now it seems strange to me that we do not receive the same pay and rations as the white soldiers. Do we not fill the same ranks?

❖❖❖

Do we not cover the same space of ground? Do we not take up
the same length of ground in a grave-yard that others do?
   —Union private Edward D. Washington, 54th (Colored) Regiment
   of the Massachusetts Volunteers, letter, March 13, 1864. (By the
   end of 1864, African-American troops began receiving equal pay.)
   [WW]

I have been one of those men who never had much confidence
in colored troops fighting, but those doubts are now all
removed, for they fought as bravely as any troops in the fort.
   —Union Colonel S. G. Hicks, on the fighting at Paducah, Kentucky,
   March 25, 1864
   [RR 8, 6]

                                  ✿

*By the late summer of 1863, both sides could see an end to the
war—for the South the vision of a Union victory was terrifying.
Jefferson Davis's predilection for using the term "slavery" to
describe the Confederacy's pending fate never seemed to have
struck the slaveholder as ironic. President Lincoln had begun to
formulate plans for "reconstruction," how and on what terms
the seceded states would return to the Union.*

Fellow citizens, no alternative is left you but victory, or subjugation, slavery and the utter ruin of yourselves, your families and
your country. The victory is within your reach.
   —Confederate President Jefferson Davis, address to the Soldiers of
   the Confederate States, August 1, 1863
   [RR 7, Doc, 388]

If I had the power, I would build up a wall of fire between
Yankeedom and the Confederate States, there to burn, for ages,
as a monument of the folly, wickedness, and vandalism of the
puritanic race! No, sir! rather than re-unite with such a people,
I would see the Confederate States desolated with fire and
sword.
   —Governor-elect of Alabama T. H. Watts, letter to Ira R. Foster on
   "reconstruction," September 12, 1863
   [RR 10, Doc, 238]

───────────❖❖❖───────────

I would make this war as severe as possible, and show no symptoms of tiring till the South begs for mercy; indeed, I know, and you know, that the end would be reached quicker by such a course than by any seeming yielding on our part. . . . The South has done her worst, and now is the time for us to pile on our blows thick and fast.

—Union Major General William Tecumseh Sherman, camp on the Big Black River, Mississippi, letter to Brigadier General J. A. Rawlins, September 17, 1863
[MS-1, 342]

Although slavery is one of the principles that we started to fight for . . . if it proves an insurmountable obstacle to the achievement of our liberty and nationality, away with it!

—*Jackson Mississippian*, newspaper editorial, September 1863
[McPherson, *What They Fought For*: ref: *The Gray and the Black*, ed. Durden, 31–32]

✿

CHICKAMAUGA AND CHATTANOOGA

After the victories at Gettysburg and Vicksburg, President Lincoln grew impatient with Union General William Rosecrans's Army of the Cumberland, which did nothing to defeat or move Confederate General Braxton Bragg's Army of Tennessee, in Chattanooga, Tennessee. Finally, on September 1, Rosecrans's army began crossing the Tennessee in preparation for an attack on Chattanooga. Bragg gave up Chattanooga and retreated south into Georgia. On September 9 Rosecrans's army took Chattanooga, and, while holding the city, then made its way after Bragg's army. Southeast of Chattanooga, near Chickamauga Creek, Rosecrans's and Bragg's armies met on September 19–20, 1863. In spite of the Confederates' victory, and Rosecrans's army's retreat to Chattanooga, it was Union Major General George Thomas ("The Rock of Chickamauga") who made a name for himself in a heroic defensive stand during the Army of the Cumberland's retreat. Bragg laid siege to Chattanooga, and though Union reinforcements arrived from Vicksburg and the Army of the Potomac, the outlook was grim

❖❖❖

for the soldiers until the arrival, a month later, of Ulysses S.
Grant, the commander of the new Division of the Mississippi. In
late November, Grant attacked and defeated Bragg's army.

Lee's army overthrown; Grant victorious. You and your noble
army now have the chance to give the finishing blow to the
rebellion. Will you neglect the chance?

—Secretary of War Edwin Stanton, letter to Major General William
Rosecrans, Commander of the Army of the Cumberland, July 7,
1863
[CW-2]

If you advance as soon as possible on them in front, while I
attack them in flank, I think we can use them up.

—Union Major General George Thomas, note to Major General
John M. Palmer, at Chickamauga, September 19, 1863
[RR 8, Poetry, 7]

I did not like to stand and be shot at without shooting back.

—Union drummer boy Johnny Clem, on why he gave up the drum
for a gun at the Battle of Chickamauga when he was twelve years
old, September 20, 1863
[BY]

We have met with a serious disaster; extent not yet ascertained.
Enemy overwhelmed us, drove our right, pierced our center,
and scattered troops there. Thomas, who had seven divisions,
remained intact at last news. Granger, with two brigades, had
gone to support Thomas on the left. Every available reserve was
used when the men stampeded.

—Union Major General William Rosecrans, telegraph message to
Washington, D.C., after Chickamauga, September 20, 1863
[CW-2]

My men are fresh, and they are just the fellows for that work.
They are raw troops and they don't know any better than to
charge up there.

—Union Brigadier General Robert Granger to Major General George
Thomas, who asked if Granger's reserve corps could drive back
Confederate forces from the ridge and enable the retreat of the army,

❖❖❖

September 20, 1863. (Granger's "fresh" men drove the Confederates back, but at the cost of half the corps suffering casualties.)
[CW-2]

We will hold this ground, or go to heaven from it.

—Union Colonel Emerson Opdycke, of Ohio, at the Battle of Chickamauga, September 20, 1863. Major General George Thomas (to be known after this date as "The Rock of Chickamauga") had just told him, "This point must be held." (Thomas's forces held the wing and enabled the Union army to withdraw to Chattanooga, around which the Confederate army then laid siege.)
[CW-2]

It was a mad irregular battle, very much resembling guerrilla warfare on a vast scale, in which one army was bushwhacking the other, and wherein all the science and the art of war went for nothing.

—Union brigadier officer, recalling Chickamauga
[NCR]

My report today is of deplorable importance. Chickamauga is as fatal a name in our history as Bull Run.

—Union observer Charles A. Dana, telegraph message, September 20, 1863
[NCR]

Our chief has done but one thing that he ought to have done since I joined his army. That was to order the attack upon the 20th. All other things he has done he ought not to have done. I am convinced that nothing but the hand of God can save us or help us as long as we have our present commander.

—Confederate General James Longstreet, letter to Secretary of War James Seddon, about General Braxton Bragg after Chickamauga, September 26, 1863
[CW-2]

We began to see things move. We felt that everything came from a plan. He came into the army quietly, no splendor, no airs, no staff. He used to go about alone. He began the campaign the

❖❖❖

moment he reached the field. Everything was done like music, everything was in harmony.

—Union officer, recollecting the changes General Ulysses S. Grant effected after relieving Rosecrans at Chattanooga
[NCR, 259]

He is confused and stunned, like a duck hit on the head, ever since Chickamauga.

—President Abraham Lincoln, to his secretary, John Hay, on General William Rosecrans, October 24, 1863. (Lincoln removed Rosecrans from his command of the Army of the Cumberland on October 19.)
[CW-2]

It looked, indeed, as if but two courses were open: one to starve, the other to surrender or be captured.

—Union Major General Ulysses S. Grant, observing the siege at Chattanooga, October 23, 1863. (Under Grant's orders, "Cracker Line" operations began October 26 to break open a shorter and safer route for supplies to the army. With food and supplies, Grant could plan for the attack of Confederate General Braxton Bragg's besieging army on Missionary Ridge.)
[CW-2]

The Cracker Line's open. Full rations, boys! Three cheers for the Cracker Line!

—Union soldiers at Chattanooga, calling out when a steamer arrived on the Tennessee River with 40,000 rations, October 30, 1863.
[CW-2]

The surgeon insisted on sending me to the hospital for treatment. I insisted on taking the field and prevailed—thinking that I had better die by rebel bullets than Union quackery.

—Union soldier M. F. Roberts, near Chattanooga, diary, 1864
[BY]

Brave men! You were ordered to go forward and take the rebel rifle-pits at the foot of these hills; you did so; and then, by the Eternal! without orders, you pushed forward and took all the

❖❖❖

enemy's works on top! Here is a fine chance for having you all court-martialed! and I myself will appear as the principal witness against you, unless you promise me one thing. ["What is it? what is it?" laughingly inquired his men.] It is that as you are now in possession of these works, you will continue, against all opposition of Bragg, Johnston, Jeff Davis, and the devil, steadfastly to hold them!

> —Union General T. J. Wood, to the soldiers who had charged past the line they were ordered to hold, and continued up the hill, where they defeated and captured Confederate General Braxton Bragg's besieging forces on Missionary Ridge, above Chattanooga, November 25, 1863. According to other sources a variation of this was said by Union Brigadier General Robert Granger. (Grant, observing the charge in the distance, had asked Granger and General George Thomas, "Who ordered those men up the ridge?" Granger explained, "They started up without orders. When those fellows get started, all hell can't stop them.")
> [RR 8, 234]

Captain, this is the death knell of the Confederacy. If we cannot cope with those fellows with the advantages we had on this line, there is not a line between here and the Atlantic Ocean where we can stop them.

> —Confederate officer, on the army's withdrawal from Missionary Ridge, November 25, 1863
> [CW-2]

I have stood your meanness as long as I intend to. You have played the part of a damned scoundrel, and are a coward, and if you were any part of a man I would slap your jaws and force you to resent it. You may as well not issue any more orders to me, for I will not obey them . . . and I say to you that if you ever again try to interfere with me or cross my path it will be at the peril of your life.

> —Confederate General Nathan Bedford Forrest, speaking to his commander, General Braxton Bragg, after the loss at Missionary Ridge, November 25, 1863
> [CW-2]

❖❖❖

No, no; mix 'em up, mix 'em up. I'm tired of states' rights.

> —Union Major General George Thomas (a native of Virginia), on the establishment of the military cemetery at Orchard Knob, a hill between Chattanooga and Missionary Ridge, when asked by a chaplain if the soldiers should be buried according to their states, November 26, 1863
> [CWT: ref: *The Life of Major General George H. Thomas*, 1882]

✿

The end of 1863 was a bad time for the South. The Confederacy was crimped geographically and economically. The Union was reestablishing itself in spite of the formidable but weary Confederate armies.

Revolver bullets flew around my head thick as hail—but not a scratch. I believe I am not to be killed by a rebel bullet.

> —Union General James Blunt, on the battle at Baxter Springs, Kansas, October 7, 1863. (Blunt lived until 1881.)
> [RR 7, 554]

Tell them that there isn't hardly enough left of me to say "I," but—hold down here a minute—tell Kate there is enough of me left to love her till I die.

> —Union soldier "Jemmy," in an Army of the Cumberland hospital, to a wounded comrade due to go home on furlough, as recorded by a nurse, B. F. Taylor, October 22, 1863
> [RR 10, 193]

Yield to the Federal authorities—to vassalage and subjugation! The bleaching of the bones of one hundred thousand gallant soldiers slain in battle would be clothed in tongues of fire to curse to everlasting infamy the man who whispers *yield*. God is with us, because He is always with the right.

> —Herschel V. Johnson, former governor of Georgia, speech at Milledgeville, Georgia, November 24, 1863
> [RR 8, 12]

❖❖❖

A cruel enemy seeks to reduce our fathers and our mothers, our wives and our children to abject slavery; to strip them of their property and drive them from their homes.
—Confederate General Robert E. Lee, announcement to his troops, advancing across the Rapidan River, Virginia, to battle with General George Meade's Army of the Potomac, November 27, 1863
[RR 8, 14]

I am too old to command this army. We should never have permitted those people to get away.
—Confederate General Robert E. Lee, to Colonel Marshall, on Meade's Army of the Potomac having retreated beyond reach, after its unsuccessful Mine Run, Virginia, campaign, December 2, 1863. (Lee usually referred to the Union army as "those people" rather than "the enemy.")
[O.R. 29, Pt. 1, 830]

If we will break up our government, dissolve the Confederacy, disband our armies, emancipate our slaves, take an oath of allegiance binding ourselves to him and to disloyalty to our states, he proposes to pardon us and not to plunder us of anything more than the property already stolen from us.
—Confederate President Jefferson Davis, on President Lincoln's amnesty offer, December 1863
[CW-2]

The President never visited the army without doing it injury; never yet that it was not followed by disaster. He was instrumental in the Gettysburg affair. He instructed Bragg at Murfreesboro. He has opened Georgia to one hundred thousand of the enemy's troops, and laid South Carolina liable to destruction. I charge him with having almost ruined the country, and will meet his champion anywhere to discuss it. Would to God he would never visit the army again!
—Confederate Congressman Henry Foote of Tennessee, on Jefferson Davis, speech before Congress, Richmond, Virginia, December 8, 1863
[RR 8, 18]

❖❖❖

We now know that the only reliable hope for peace is the vigor of our resistance, while the cessation of their hostility is only to be expected from the pressure of their necessities.

—Confederate President Jefferson Davis, to his Congress, December 8, 1863
[CW-2]

If God Almighty had yet in store another plague worse than all the others which he intended to have let loose on the Egyptians in case Pharaoh still hardened his heart, I am sure it must have been a regiment or so of half-armed, half-disciplined Confederate Cavalry.

—North Carolina Governor Zebulon Vance, letter to Confederate Secretary of War James Seddon, on the government's lack of wisdom in having authorized guerilla cavalrymen, who often plundered the Southern towns they rode through, December 1863
[JR]

To secure the safety of the navigation of the Mississippi River, I would slay millions. On that point I am not only insane, but mad. . . . For every bullet shot at a steamboat, I would shoot a thousand 300-pounder Parrotts into even helpless towns on Red, Ouachita, Yazoo, or wherever a boat can float or soldier march.

—Union Major General William Tecumseh Sherman, letter to General John Logan, on hearing that guerillas were shooting at steamboats on the Mississippi River, near Vicksburg, December 21, 1863
[CW-2]

❖❖❖

1864

*Though the previous year's battles had seemed horrific, the
fighting and killing in 1864 was to be worse. The armies were
quiet this winter, however. In January in the U.S. Senate, John
Henderson of Missouri proposed the Thirteenth Amendment to
the Constitution, whereby slavery would be outlawed throughout the Union. In April, the Senate approved the Thirteenth
Amendment. (The House of Representatives did not approve the
amendment until January 31, 1865, and it did not become law
until December 1865.) Union Major General William Tecumseh
Sherman, commander of the Army of the Tennessee, ever forth-
right about his loathing of Confederate rationale for the war,
would become, by year's end, the Union's most important general after Lieutenant General Grant, and, in the Confederacy,
the most hated.*

Madam, my soldiers have to subsist themselves even if the
whole country must be ruined to maintain them. There are two
armies here. One is in rebellion against the Union; the other is
fighting for the Union. If either must starve to death, I propose
it shall not be the army that is loyal.

> —Union Major General William Tecumseh Sherman, to a woman
> in Tennessee who objected to his army taking food, early 1864
> [CW-3]

If they want eternal war, well and good; we accept the issue, and
will dispossess them and put our friends in their places. . . .
Three years ago, by a little reflection and patience, they could
have had a hundred years of peace and prosperity, but they pre-

ferred war; very well. . . . Next year their lands will be taken; for
in war we can take them, and rightfully, too, and in another year
they may beg in vain for their lives.

—Union Major General William Tecumseh Sherman, from
Vicksburg, Mississippi, letter to Major Roswell M. Sawyer, assistant
adjutant general of Sherman's army, Huntsville, Alabama, January
31, 1864. (Sherman suggested the long letter from which this quotation has been extracted be published as "a warning to the civilians
in his southward path." He wrote his brother, appending a copy, "Its
publication would do no harm, except to turn the Richmond press
against me as the prince of barbarians.")
[RR 8]

We are not in a condition, and never have been, in my opinion,
to invade the enemy's country with a prospect of permanent
benefit.

—Confederate General Robert E. Lee, letter to Confederate
President Jefferson Davis, early February 1864
[O.R. Vol. 33, Pt. 1, 1144]

Daughters of Georgia, I still need socks. Requisitions for them
are daily pouring in upon me. I still have yarn to furnish you. I
earnestly desire to secure a pair of socks for every barefooted
soldier from Georgia.

—Quartermaster-General of Georgia Ira R. Foster, letter "To the
Women of Georgia," Atlanta, February 5, 1864
[RR 8, Poetry, 48]

Now, God damn you, go back to the front and fight! You might
as well be killed there as here, for if you ever run away again
you'll not get off so easy.

—Confederate Major General Nathan Bedford Forrest to a fleeing
soldier, near West Point, Mississippi, February 21, 1864
[CW-2]

Surrender, you damned rebels, or I'll shoot you!

—Union Colonel Ulric Dahlgren, moments before he was
ambushed and shot dead by Confederate General Fitz Lee's soldiers, at King and Queen Courthouse, Virginia, March 3, 1864.
(Dahlgren and his raiders meant to sweep into Richmond and assas-
sinate Confederate President Davis and his cabinet. "Once in the

❖❖❖

city it must be destroyed, and Jeff Davis and cabinet killed. Pioneers will go along with combustible material," read a note that the Confederates insisted Dahlgren wrote. Union officials believed the Confederates had fabricated this note to justify the mutilation of Dahlgren's corpse.)
[CW-2]

They have taken one hundred thousand negroes, which cost half a million of whites four thousand millions of dollars, and now seek to repudiate self-government—subjugate Southern people, and confiscate their property.
—Georgia Governor Joseph E. Brown, on the emancipation of slaves, annual message read before the Georgia State Legislature, March 10, 1864
[RR 8, 51]

If we can break up the enemy's arrangements early, and throw him back, he will not be able to recover his position or his morale until the Presidential election is over, and then we shall have a new President to treat with. If Lincoln has any success early he will be able to get more men and may be able to secure his own re-election. In that event the war must go on for four years longer.
—Confederate General James Longstreet, from Headquarters, Greeneville, East Tennessee, to General A. R. Lawton, Quartermaster-General, Richmond, Virginia, on the Confederacy's hopes for a Democrat to replace President Lincoln, March 5, 1864. (Longstreet hoped to persuade Lawton to "make arrangements for supplying us abundantly with corn, etc., by stopping the use of the railroad for any other than army purposes for forty days.")
[O.R. Series 1, Vol. 32, Pt. 3, 588]

✿

ULYSSES S. GRANT

Though seemingly an unlikely figure to rise to the highest military rank, Lieutenant General, Ulysses S. Grant (a West Point graduate and Mexican War veteran who was working in his father's store in Illinois when the war began), was the com-

❖❖❖

manding general President Lincoln had always been looking for.
He was aggressive and straightforward, but sometimes, as he in
his honesty would admit, aggressive to a fault in the case of
assaults at Vicksburg and, this spring, at Cold Harbor, Virginia.
Though becoming commander in chief of all the Union armies
with his appointment as Lieutenant General, he was with the
Army of the Potomac "in the field," as he pursued and attacked
and blocked Lee's Army of Northern Virginia until that great
Confederate general's surrender in April 1865.

He doesn't ask me to do impossibilities for him, and he's the first
general I've had that didn't!

   —President Abraham Lincoln, speaking of General Ulysses S.
Grant, according to the journalist William O. Stoddard
[IWH]

Not a great man except morally; not an original or brilliant man,
but sincere, thoughtful, deep, and gifted with courage that
never faltered.

   —Union Assistant Secretary of War Charles A. Dana, on General
Ulysses S. Grant
[CW-2]

Find out where your enemy is. Get at him as soon as you can,
and strike him as hard as you can. And keep moving on.

   —Union General Ulysses S. Grant, reply to being asked to describe
his war strategy
[CW-3]

With this high honor devolves upon you also a corresponding
responsibility. As the country herein trusts you, so, under God,
it will sustain you.

   —President Abraham Lincoln, presenting Ulysses S. Grant with his
commission as Lieutenant General, in the president's cabinet
chamber, March 9, 1864 (this commission became official on March
10).
[RR 8, Diary, 50]

❖❖❖

The chief characteristic in your nature is the simple faith in success you have always manifested, which I can liken to nothing else than the faith a Christian has in his Savior.

—Union Major General William Tecumseh Sherman, letter to Lieutenant General Ulysses S. Grant, March 10, 1864
[CW-2]

Lee's army will be your objective point. Wherever Lee goes, there you will go also.

—Union Lt. General Ulysses S. Grant, letter to General George Meade, commanding Army of the Potomac, from Culpeper Court House, Virginia, April 9, 1864
[USG]

The Army of the Potomac is in splendid condition and evidently feels like whipping somebody. I feel much better with this command than I did before seeing it.

—Union Lt. General Ulysses S. Grant, letter to Major General Henry Halleck, April 26, 1864
[USG]

The particulars of your plans I neither know nor seek to know. You are vigilant and self-reliant, and pleased with this, I wish not to obtrude any restraints or constraints upon you. While I am very anxious that any great disaster, or capture of our men in great numbers, shall be avoided, I know that these points are less likely to escape your attention than they would mine.

—President Abraham Lincoln, letter to Lt. General Ulysses S. Grant, from Washington, D.C., to Army Headquarters, Culpeper Court House, Virginia, April 30, 1864
[RR 9, Poetry, 5]

We must make up our minds to get into line of battle and to stay there, for that man will fight us every day and every hour till the end of the war.

—Confederate General James Longstreet, to "visitors" at Gordonsville, about his former friend Union General Ulysses S. Grant, and Grant's campaign, the seventh to be attempted by the Union army, to take Richmond, late April–early May 1864
[CW-3]

❖❖❖

FORT PILLOW MASSACRE

Though revered and admired by many then and now, not least by Shelby Foote, the author of the marvelous The Civil War: A Narrative, *Nathan Bedford Forrest, the bane of the Union forces in the South, and unarguably the greatest cavalry general of the Confederacy, was, before the war, a wealthy Mississippi planter and slave-trader and, after the war, a founder of the Ku Klux Klan. The testimony concerning his participation in and encouragement of the massacre of surrendered African-American soldiers at Fort Pillow, Tennessee, in the spring of 1864, would seem to convict him and his troops of mass murder.*

Should my demand be refused, I cannot be responsible for the fate of your command.

—Confederate Major General Nathan Bedford Forrest, note to the Union commander, Major William Bradford, of Fort Pillow, Tennessee, demanding surrender, April 12, 1864. "I will not surrender," was Bradford's reply. Forrest stormed the fort and sixty-three percent of the Union force was killed or wounded, with many of the African-American troops executed upon surrender.
[CW-3]

Boys, it is only death, any how; if you don't go out they will come in and carry you out.

—Union soldiers to the "Colored" troops, at Fort Pillow, after the surrender to the forces of Confederate General Nathan Bedford Forrest, according to African-American soldier Manuel Nichols, April 12, 1864. (Nichols was shot in the arm and the head, but survived.)
[RR 8, 14]

"Kill 'em, kill 'em; God damn 'em; that's Forrest's orders, not to leave one alive." I saw four white men and at least twenty-five negroes shot while begging for mercy.

—Union African-American soldier William F. Mays, recalling the Fort Pillow massacre
[RR 8, 29, 71]

❖❖❖

The river was dyed with the blood of the slaughtered for two hundred yards. The approximate loss was upward of five hundred killed, but few of the officers escaping. My loss was about twenty killed. It is hoped that these facts will demonstrate to the Northern people that Negro soldiers cannot cope with Southerners.

—Confederate Major General Nathan Bedford Forrest, dispatch on the Fort Pillow massacre, April 12, 1864
[USG]

It is not the policy or the interest of the South to destroy the negro, on the contrary to preserve and protect him, and all who have surrendered to us have received kind and humane treatment.

—Confederate Major General Nathan Bedford Forrest, letter, June 20, 1864, in reply to Union Major General Cadwallader C. Washburn, who charged him with the murder of surrendered "Colored" soldiers at Fort Pillow.
[RR 10, 724]

When I went into the war, I meant to fight. Fighting means killing.

—Confederate Major General Nathan Bedford Forrest, having been asked a few days after the end of the war by former Union general staff member Bryan McAlister about the Fort Pillow massacre.
[RR 8, Poetry, 56]

❖

BATTLES OF THE WILDERNESS AND SPOTSYLVANIA COURT HOUSE

"My general plan now," Lieutenant General Ulysses S. Grant wrote in his Memoirs *about the spring of 1864 campaign, "was to concentrate all the forces possible against the Confederate armies in the field." In Virginia, the Army of the Potomac, under Meade's command but under Grant's supervision, crossed the Rappahannock River and set out for battle with Lee's outnumbered and under-supplied Army of Northern Virginia. The*

❖❖❖

campaign in Virginia started May 4, 1864, and would not end until the following April, upon Lee's surrender. The Wilderness, dense with woods and bushes and with creeks running through it, was the unfortunate site for Grant's army to await its supply trains. After three days of battle in the woods, culminating in brush fires that killed some of the wounded, in all which the Union army suffered terrific casualties, Grant pushed to get the fighting out into the open, where the Army of the Potomac could take better advantage of its superior numbers, and to head for Richmond. But Lee countered and blocked the Union forces from the crossroads called Spotsylvania Court House. On May 8 the Battle of Spotsylvania began, culminating in the fight at the "Bloody Angle of Spotsylvania," on May 12, where there were at least 10,000 casualties. Not being able to drive through Lee's army, Grant directed his army around to the left, southeast. The Union suffered 33,000 casualties before they were clear of the Wilderness and Spotsylvania, far more than the Confederates, but the Southern armies did not have replacements as Grant's did.

We are playing right into these devils' hands! Bushwacking is the game! There ain't a tree in our front, twenty feet high, but there is a Reb up that tree!

—Union soldier Wad Rider, Battle of the Wilderness, May 5, 1864
[BG, 980: ref: Warren Goss, *Recollections of a Private*]

Battle be damned! It ain't no battle. It's a worse riot than Chickamauga was! You Yanks don't call this a battle, do you? At Chickamauga there was at least a rear, but here there ain't neither front nor rear. It's all a damned mess! And our two armies ain't nothin' but howlin' mobs.

—Confederate private from Texas, wounded and captured by the Union, and questioned about the fighting in the Wilderness, May 5–6, 1864
[BG, 977: ref: Buell, "The Cannoneer," 1890]

❖❖❖

Hit hard when you start, but don't start until you have everything ready.
> —Confederate General James Longstreet, remark to Lieutenant
> Colonel G. Moxley Sorrel, Battle of the Wilderness, May 6, 1864
> [CW-3]

When you go in there, I wish you to give those men the cold steel—they will stand and fire all day, and never move, unless you charge them.
> —Confederate General Robert E. Lee, to General John Gregg, of
> the Texas Brigade, May 6, 1864
> [BG, 983: ref: R.C. (anonymous), *The Land We Love*, 1868]

Oh, I am heartily tired of hearing about what *Lee* is going to do. Some of you always seem to think he is suddenly going to turn a double somersault and land in our rear and on both our flanks at the same time. Go back to your command and try to think what we are going to do ourselves, instead of what *Lee* is going to do.
> —Union Lt. General Ulysses S. Grant, to a brigadier general who
> rode to him to say Lee was doing the same as Stonewall Jackson had
> done a year before, during Chancellorsville, May 6, 1864
> [CW-3]

I could have caught a pot full of [bullets] if I had had a strong iron vessel rigged on a pole as a butterfly net.
> —Union soldier Frank Wilkeson, about the Battle of the
> Wilderness
> [BY]

It was a series of fierce attacks and repulses on either side, and the hostile lines swayed back and forth over a strip of ground from 200 yards to a mile in width on which the severely wounded of both sides were scattered. This strip of woods was on fire in many places, and some wounded, unable to escape, were thus either suffocated or burned to death. The number who thus perished is unknown, but it is supposed to have been about 200. The stretcher bearers of the Ambulance Corps followed the line of battle closely, and displayed great gallantry

❖❖❖

in their efforts to bring off the wounded lying between the lines, but with very small success, it being almost impossible to find wounded men lying scattered through the dense thickets, and the enemy firing at every moving light, or even at the slightest noise.
> —Union officer McParlin, official medical report after the Battle of the Wilderness, May 7, 1864
> [CWM, 129]

I do not know of any way to put down this Rebellion and restore the authority of the government except by fighting, and fighting means that men must be killed. If the people of this country expect that the war can be conducted to a successful issue in any other way than by fighting, they must get somebody other than myself to command the army.
> —Union Lt. General Ulysses S. Grant, to a newspaper reporter, Spotsylvania Court House, Virginia, May 10, 1864
> [WW]

I am now sending back to Belle Plain all my wagons for a fresh supply of provisions and ammunition, and purpose to fight it out on this line if it takes all summer.
> —Union Lt. General Ulysses S. Grant, note to Major General Henry Halleck, chief of staff of the Army, from near Spotsylvania Court House, Virginia, May 11, 1864
> [CW-3]

General Lee, you shall not lead my men in a charge. No man can do that, sir. Another is here for that purpose. These men behind you are Georgians, Virginians, and Carolinians. They have never failed you on any field. They will not fail you here. Will you, boys? . . . General Lee, you must go to the rear.
> —Confederate General John Brown Gordon, to General Lee, who proposed leading the charge against Union General Winfield Hancock's forces at "the Bloody Angle," Spotsylvania Court House, May 12, 1864
> [BG, 999: ref: Gordon, *Reminiscences of the Civil War*, 1903]

————— ❖❖❖ —————

I never expect to be believed when I tell of what I saw of the horrors of Spotsylvania, because I should be loath to believe it myself were the cases reversed.

—Union officer, about the fighting in "the Bloody Angle," Spotsylvania, Virginia, May 12, 1864
[CW-3]

We have met a man this time, who either does not know when he is whipped, or who cares not if he loses his whole Army.

—Confederate observer, after Spotsylvania, on Union Lt. General Ulysses S. Grant's military tactics
[CWDD, 500]

We must destroy this army of Grant's before he gets to James River. If he gets there it will become a siege, and then it will be a mere question of time.

—Confederate General Robert E. Lee, to General Jubal Early, late May 1864. Lee could defensively counter Grant's army, but he could not defeat or destroy it. (By late June, there was an effective siege of the important city of Petersburg, Virginia, and surrender did become "a mere question of time.")
[CW-3]

✿

COLD HARBOR

Grant continued to try to get the Army of the Potomac around or through Lee's Army of Northern Virginia. As Lee countered Grant's moves, the Union's persistence wore the Confederate ranks thinner and the distance from Richmond shorter. Cold Harbor (not a harbor at all but a crossroads north of the Chickahominy River) became the site of a futile assault by Grant's forces, on June 3, 1864. From Cold Harbor, Grant moved his army across the James River to undertake the siege of Petersburg, the railroad hub of Virginia south of Richmond.

❖❖❖

It seemed more like a volcanic blast than a battle, and was just about as destructive.

—Union soldier, New Hampshire Volunteers, letter, of the battle at Cold Harbor, June 3, 1864
[NHV]

I was struck by a musket ball directly over the heart so severely that I was knocked over and lay in a senseless condition for some time; my life being saved by my roll book, diary and my wife's picture. . . . Our company went into the engagement forty-eight strong and came out with three fit for duty.

—Union Sergeant Solon Greenleaf Blaisdell, 12th Regiment, New Hampshire Volunteers, Company F, recollection of the battle at Cold Harbor, June 3, 1864
[NHV]

Into such a scalding cauldron did the brave Colonel Steadman, using a ramrod for a sword, lead four regiments of his brigade, massed in column by division and led by the Twelfth New Hampshire in the early light of that fatal morn. In less than ten minutes from the word "forward" there was no brigade to be seen, and of its leading regiment nearly one half lay dead or disabled on the field.

—Union Captain Asa W. Bartlett, remembering Cold Harbor
[NHV, 202]

I am disgusted with the generalship displayed. Our men have, in many instances, been foolishly and wantonly sacrificed. Assault after assault has been ordered upon the enemy's intrenchments when they knew nothing about the strength or position of the enemy.

—Union Colonel Emory Upton, letter to his sister, from Cold Harbor, Virginia, June 4, 1864
[BG, 1002: ref: *The Life and Letters of Emory Upton*, 1885]

I have always regretted that the last assault at Cold Harbor was ever made. . . . At Cold Harbor no advantage whatever was gained to compensate for the heavy loss we sustained.
—Union Lt. General Ulysses S. Grant, reflecting on the disastrous attack at Cold Harbor, June 3, 1864
[USG]

Now we will rest the men and use the spade for their protection until a new vein has been struck.
—Union Lt. General Ulysses S. Grant, letter to Major General George Meade, after Cold Harbor, from City Point, Virginia, June 18, 1864
[O.R. Series 1, Vol. 40, Pt. 2, 156]

We accepted this war for an object, a worthy object, and the war will end when that object is attained. Under God, I hope it never will until that time.
—President Abraham Lincoln, speech at the Great Central Sanitary Fair, Philadelphia, June 16, 1864
[CW-3]

What is all this struggling and fighting for? This ruin and death to thousands of families? . . . What advancement of mankind to compensate for the present horrible calamities?
—Mrs. Sarah Butler, letter to her husband in Virginia, Union General Benjamin Butler, June 19, 1864
[BCF]

These last few days have been very bad. Many a man has gone crazy since this campaign began from the terrible pressure on mind and body.
—Union Captain Oliver Wendell Holmes, Jr., letter to his parents, on the first two months of Grant's campaign in Virginia, June 24, 1864
[OWH, 149]

❖❖❖

His talent and strategy consists in accumulating overwhelming numbers.
  —Confederate General Robert E. Lee, on Union Lt. General Ulysses S. Grant, in a letter to one of Lee's sons, July 1864
  [CW-3]

I have seen your dispatch expressing your unwillingness to break your hold where you are. Neither am I willing. Hold on with a bulldog grip, and chew and choke as much as possible.
  —President Abraham Lincoln, telegram to Lt. General Ulysses S. Grant, August 17, 1864. Reading this, Grant observed to staff members, "The President has more nerve than any of his advisers."
  [CW-3]

✿

WAR AT SEA

Far across the Atlantic Ocean, off the coast of France in the English Channel, the vexatious C.S.S. Alabama, which had sunk or taken at least sixty-five Union ships over the past two years, met the U.S.S. Kearsarge.

The contest will no doubt be contested and obstinate, but the two ships are so evenly matched that I do not feel at liberty to decline it. God defend the right, and have mercy upon the souls of those who fall, as many of us must.
  —Confederate Captain Raphael Semmes, June 18, 1864, on the next day's battle between his *Alabama* and Captain John A. Winslow's U.S.S. *Kearsarge,* off the coast of Cherbourg, France
  [CW-3]

The name of your ship has become a household word wherever civilization extends. Shall that name be tarnished by defeat? The thing is impossible. Remember that you are in the English Channel, the theater of so much of the naval glory of our race. The eyes of all Europe are at this moment upon you.
  —Confederate Captain Raphael Semmes, to his officers and sailors, as the *Alabama* sailed out to meet the *Kearsarge,* June 19, 1864
  [BG, 875: ref: John M. Kell, *Recollections of a Naval Life,* 1900]

———————— ❖❖❖ ————————

It was the same thing as if two men were to go out and fight a duel, and one of them, unknown to the other, were to put on a suit of mail under his outer garment.
—Confederate Captain Raphael Semmes, complaining after his *Alabama* was defeated that the *Kearsarge* was chain-armored [CW-3]

Let her have the steam; we had better blow her to hell than to let the Yankees whip us!
—Confederate assistant engineer Matt O'Brien, of the *Alabama*, to a chief engineer, in the midst of the battle, June 19, 1864 [BG, 876: ref: John M. Kell, *Recollections of a Naval Life*, 1900]

A noble Roman once stabbed his daughter, rather than she should be polluted by the foul embrace of a tyrant. It was with a similar feeling that Kell and I saw the *Alabama* go down. We had buried her as we had christened her, and she was safe from the polluting touch of the hated Yankee!
—Confederate Captain Raphael Semmes, reflecting on having scuttled the *Alabama* after the fight with the *Kearsarge* [CW-3]

◊

THE ATLANTA CAMPAIGN

While Grant directed operations against the Confederacy in Virginia, he left Major General William Tecumseh Sherman, whom he knew well and respected, to his own devices in the campaign against Atlanta and General Joseph Johnston's Army of Tennessee. One purpose of the campaign, in fact, was to keep General Johnston from being able to afford sending off any of his troops to aid General Lee. The Atlanta campaign took months, with distractions and worries for Sherman to the north and south, including the irrepressible Confederate cavalry General Nathan Bedford Forrest, who threatened supply lines. In July Johnston lost his command in spite of maintaining a sensible and effective defensive strategy against Sherman's larger forces. Jefferson Davis replaced him with General John B. Hood, who was indeed more aggressive than Johnston, but who lost many more men as well as the city of Atlanta on September 2. Sherman's army set out on its March to the Sea on November 15, leaving everything but the houses and churches in Atlanta destroyed.

You I propose to move against Johnston's army, to break it up and to get into the interior of the enemy's country as far as you can, inflicting all the damage you can against their war resources. I do not propose to lay down for you a plan of campaign, but simply lay down the work it is desirable to have done and leave you free to execute it in your own way.

—Union Lt. General Ulysses S. Grant, letter from Washington, D.C., to Union Major General William Tecumseh Sherman, commanding the Military Division of the Mississippi, April 4, 1864 [MS-II, 26]

Georgia has a million of inhabitants. If they can live, we should not starve.

—Union General William Tecumseh Sherman, letter from Nashville to Lt. General Ulysses S. Grant, in Washington, D.C., on Sherman's idea to advance without supply lines, April 10, 1864 [MS-II, 28]

In this army, one hole in the seat of the breeches indicates a captain, two holes a lieutenant, and the seat of the pants all out indicates that the individual is a private.

—Confederate soldier Sebron Sneed, letter to his wife, from near Atlanta, June 7, 1864 [JR]

There never will be peace in Tennessee till Forrest is dead.

—Union General William Tecumseh Sherman, letter to Secretary of War Edwin Stanton in Washington, D.C., from "in the field," June 15, 1864. Sherman issued orders to hunt down Confederate General Nathan Bedford Forrest, whose cavalry threatened the supply routes along the railroads. [O.R. Ser 1, Vol 39, Pt. 2, 121]

The whole country is one vast fort, and Johnston must have at least fifty miles of connected trenches, with abatis and finished batteries. We gain ground daily, fighting all the time.
—Union Major General William Tecumseh Sherman, telegraph message to Major General Henry Halleck, Washington, D.C., June 23, 1864
[MS-II, 59]

Fighting is the least part of a general's work. The battle will fight itself.
—Union Major General William Tecumseh Sherman, before the battle at Kennesaw Mountain, June 27, 1864
[CW-3]

They seemed to walk up and take death as coolly as if they were automatic or wooden men.
—Confederate soldier, on the Union attack at Kennesaw Mountain, led by generals Jeff Davis and John Newton, on Confederate General Benjamin Cheatham's division, at "the Dead Angle," June 27, 1864. (This assault on Johnston's dug-in troops was, wrote Sherman, "the hardest fight of the campaign up to that date." There were 2,500 casualties from his ranks.)
[CW-3]

I begin to regard the death and mangling of a couple of thousand men as a small affair, a kind of morning dash. It may well be that we become hardened. . . . The worst of the war is not yet begun.
—Union Major General George Thomas, letter to his wife, after the Battle at Kennesaw Mountain, June 29, 1864
[CW-3]

One thing is certain, the enemy cannot remain long where he is. He must come out, and when he does, all I ask or wish is to be turned loose with my command. . . . I will be on all sides of him, attacking day and night. He shall not cook a meal or have a night's sleep, and I will wear his army to a frazzle before he gets out of the country.
—Confederate Major General Nathan Bedford Forrest, letter to General Robert E. Lee, about Union General Andrew Jackson

❖❖❖

Smith's cavalry, occupying Harrisburg, near Tupelo, Mississippi, July 13, 1864. (Forrest was shot in the big toe on July 15 and had to give up command as Smith defeated Forrest's and General Stephen Lee's forces.)
[CW-3]

From a close observation of his career, I became persuaded that his nervous dread of losing a battle would prevent at all times his ability to cope with an enemy of nearly equal strength, and that opportunities would thus constantly be lost which under other commanders would open a plain path to victory.

—Confederate Secretary of State Judah P. Benjamin, letter, on General Joseph Johnston, July 1864. (Benjamin suggested to President Jefferson Davis that Johnston be removed from his command of the Army of Tennessee even while defending Atlanta from Sherman's forces.)
[CW-3]

As the enemy has double our number, we must be on the defensive. My plan of operations must, therefore, depend on that of the enemy. It is mainly to watch for an opportunity to fight to advantage.

—Confederate General Joseph Johnston, reply to President Jefferson Davis's request for "specific information," on his plans for defeating Sherman's forces outside Atlanta, July 16, 1864. (Johnston was removed from command the next day.)
[CW-3]

I cannot guess his movements as I could those of Johnston, who was a sensible man and only did sensible things.

—Union Major General William Tecumseh Sherman, letter to General Henry Slocum, on Confederate General John B. Hood, who had replaced General Joseph Johnston as commander of the Army of Tennessee
[CW-3]

❖❖❖

I expected something to happen to Grant and me; either the rebels or the newspapers would kill us both, and I looked to McPherson as the man to follow us and finish the war.
> —Union Major General William Tecumseh Sherman, in conversation with a friend after hearing General James McPherson had been killed in the Battle of Atlanta, July 22, 1864
> [CW-3]

Sometimes a bullet comes a little too near where I am writing and makes me spoil a letter; a man never gets so used to them but what he will dodge when they whistle past his ear.
> —Union soldier John Moulton, letter to his mother, from near Atlanta, August 7, 1864
> [BY]

This place is to the Confederacy as important as the heart is to the body. We must hold it.
> —Georgia Governor Joseph E. Brown, about Atlanta, letter to Confederate President Jefferson Davis
> [CW-3]

We keep hammering away all the time, and there is no peace, inside or outside Atlanta. . . . One thing is certain, whether we get inside of Atlanta or not, it will be a used-up community when we are done with it.
> —Union Major General William Tecumseh Sherman, telegraph message to Major General Henry Halleck, August 7, 1864
> [MS-2]

Let us destroy Atlanta, and make it a desolation.
> —Union Major General William Tecumseh Sherman, note to General Oliver Howard, August 10, 1864
> [CW-3]

I have Atlanta as certainly as if it were in my hand!
> —Union Major General William Tecumseh Sherman, August 30, 1864
> [CW-3]

❖❖❖

The fortunes of war have placed the city of Atlanta in your hands.
  —Atlanta Mayor James M. Calhoun, surrendering to the commander of Union General Henry Slocum's lead division of Sherman's army, September 2, 1864
  [CW-3]

If the people raise a howl against my barbarity and cruelty, I will answer that war is war, and not popularity-seeking. If they want peace, they and their relatives must stop the war.
  —Union Major General William Tecumseh Sherman, letter to Major General Henry Halleck, September 4, 1864
  [CW-3]

. . . permit me to say that the unprecedented measure you propose transcends, in studied and ingenious cruelty, all acts ever before brought to my attention in the dark history of war. In the name of God and humanity, I protest, believing that you will find that you are expelling from their homes and firesides the wives and children of a brave people.
  —Confederate General John B. Hood, letter to Union Major General William Tecumseh Sherman, on Sherman's order for the evacuation of Atlanta, September 9, 1864
  [CW-3]

In the name of common sense, I ask you not to appeal to a just God in such a sacrilegious manner. You who, in the midst of peace and prosperity, have plunged a nation into war—dark and cruel war—who dared and badgered us to battle, insulted our flag, seized our arsenals and forts. . . . Talk thus to the marines, but not to me, who have seen these things. . . .
  —Union Major General William Tecumseh Sherman, reply to Confederate General John B. Hood, September 10, 1864
  [CW-3]

War is cruelty, and you cannot refine it; and those who brought war on the country deserve all the curses and maledictions a people can pour out. . . . You might as well appeal against the thunderstorm as against these terrible hardships of war. They

❖❖❖

are inevitable, and the only way the people of Atlanta can hope once more to live in peace and quiet at home is to stop this war which can alone be done by admitting that it began in error and is perpetuated in pride. . . . I want peace, and believe it can only be reached through Union and war, and I will ever conduct war purely with a view to perfect and early success.

—Union Major General William Tecumseh Sherman, reply to the mayor and city council of Atlanta, September 12, 1864, who objected to his order for the evacuation of all civilians from the city [UR]

The end has come, no doubt of the fact. Our Army has so moved as to uncover Macon and Augusta. We are going to be wiped off the face of the earth.

—Mary Boykin Chesnut, wife of Confederate Brigadier General James Chesnut, diary, September 21, 1864 [CCW, 648]

I believe it is in the power of the men of the Confederacy to plant our banners on the banks of the Ohio, where we shall say to the Yankee: "Be quiet, or we shall teach you another lesson."

—Confederate President Jefferson Davis, speech, Columbia, South Carolina, October 4, 1864 [CW-3]

All the pictures and verbal descriptions of hell I have ever seen never gave me half so vivid an idea of it as did this flame-wrapped city tonight.

—Union officer, on the sight of Atlanta as it burned, November 15, 1864 [CW-3]

❖

THE BATTLE OF MOBILE BAY

In the Deep South, blockading Mobile Bay was another Union goal in the summer of 1864. The serious obstacles to the blockade outside the bay were Forts Morgan, Powell, and Gaines. Within the bay was the Confederacy's new ironclad ram, the Tennessee.

❖❖❖

I never found that I needed rum to enable me to do my duty. I will order two cups of good coffee to each man at 2 o'clock, and at 8 o'clock I will pipe all hands to breakfast in Mobile Bay.

—Admiral David Farragut, August 4, 1864, in reply to being asked if he and his men would require alcohol in preparation for the next day's Battle of Mobile Bay. (The battle, won by Farragut's ships, ended at 10 A.M.)
[CW-3]

It is a curious sight to catch a single shot from so heavy a piece of ordnance. First you see the puff of white smoke upon the distant ramparts, and then you see the shot coming, looking exactly as if some gigantic hand has thrown in play a ball toward you. By the time it is half way, you get the boom of the report, and then the howl of the missile, which apparently grows so rapidly in size that every green hand on board who can see it is certain that it will hit him between the eyes. Then, as it goes past with a shriek like a thousand devils, the inclination to do reverence is so strong that it is almost impossible to resist it.

—Union surgeon, on the shots fired from Fort Morgan, Mobile Bay, Alabama, on Farragut's passing fleet, August 5, 1864
[CW-3]

Everybody has taken it into their heads that one ship can whip a dozen, and if the trial is not made, we who are in her are damned for life; consequently, the trial must be made. So goes the world.

—Confederate Admiral Franklin Buchanan, note to a friend, about his new flagship, the ironclad ram *Tennessee*
[CW-3]

Do the best you can, sir, and when all is done, surrender.

—Confederate Admiral Franklin Buchanan, to Commander James D. Johnston of the *Tennessee,* August 5, 1864
[CW-3]

❖❖❖

Damn the torpedoes! Full speed ahead!

—Union Admiral David Farragut, in spite of the previous ship, the *Tecumseh*, blowing up after hitting a torpedo (a floating mine), during the Battle of Mobile Bay, Alabama, August 5, 1864. (Farragut's fleet and a Union land force took the Mobile Bay forts and effectively began the blockade of the port. General Canby captured the city the following spring.)
[CW-3]

✿

THE REELECTION OF ABRAHAM LINCOLN

Lincoln's nemesis George B. McClellan was the Democratic nominee for president. The war was not going well enough or fast enough to suit the nation, which many in the Confederacy saw as a blessing. Whoever replaced Lincoln as president would be more likely to negotiate with the South for peace and independence. President Lincoln was easily reelected November 8.

I feel compelled to drop you a line concerning the political condition of the country as it strikes me. I am in active correspondence with your staunchest friends in every state, and from them all I hear but one report. The tide is setting strongly against us.

—Henry J. Raymond, *New York Times* editor, letter to President Lincoln on Lincoln's reelection chances, August 23, 1864
[CW-3]

This morning, as for some days past, it seems exceedingly probable that this Administration will not be reelected. Then it will be my duty to so cooperate with the President-elect as to save the Union between the election and the inauguration; as he will have secured his election on such ground that he cannot possibly save it afterwards.

—President Abraham Lincoln, memorandum, August 23, 1864
[CW-3]

❖❖❖

I am going to be beaten, and unless some great change takes place *badly* beaten.
—President Abraham Lincoln, on the coming presidential election, August 1864. (This "great change" took place, most notably with Sherman's taking of Atlanta in early September.)
[BCF]

For my country's sake, I deplore the result.
—Democratic presidential candidate George B. McClellan, on having lost the election of 1864 to Abraham Lincoln
[CWDD, 594]

Human nature will not change. In any future great national trial, compared with the men of this, we shall have as weak and as strong; as silly and as wise; as bad and as good. Let us therefore study the incidents of this, as philosophy to learn wisdom from, and none of them as wrongs to be revenged.
—President Abraham Lincoln, "Response to Serenade" congratulating him on his reelection, November 10, 1864
[CW-3]

I feel how weak and fruitless must be any words of mine which should attempt to beguile you from the grief of a loss so overwhelming. But I cannot refrain from tendering to you the consolation that may be found in the thanks of the Republic they died to save.
—President Abraham Lincoln, letter to Mrs. Lydia Bixby, the mother of two sons (not five as Lincoln believed) killed in battle, November 21, 1864
[GS, 105; CWDD, 599]

❋

SHERIDAN'S SHENANDOAH VALLEY CAMPAIGN

Union General Philip Sheridan was named commander of the newly formed Army of the Shenandoah on August 7, 1864, in order to drive Confederate General Jubal Early out of the Shenandoah Valley. (Early had threatened Baltimore, Maryland, and Washington, D.C., in July.) In September he defeated Early in two battles, at Winchester and Fishers Hill, Virginia. On the morning of October 19, however, Early's men attacked Sheridan's camp at Cedar Creek, Virginia. Sheridan was away, having been in Washington, D.C., but returned in time to rally his men to defeat Early's.

The people must be left nothing but their eyes to weep with over the war.

> —Union General Philip Sheridan, on the Shenandoah Valley Campaign, wherein Lt. General Ulysses S. Grant ordered him to turn the region into a "barren waste," September 1864
> [BCF]

We might as well whip them today. If we don't, we shall have to do it tomorrow. Sheridan will get it out of us sometime.

> —Union General William Emory, having received General Philip Sheridan's orders to be ready to resist Confederate General Jubal Early's forces at Winchester, Virginia, September 19, 1864
> [CW-3]

We just sent them whirling through Winchester, and we are after them tomorrow. This army behaved splendidly.

> —Union General Philip Sheridan, telegram to Secretary of War Edwin Stanton, after the defeat of Confederate General Jubal Early's forces at Winchester, September 20, 1864
> [OR, Series 1, Vol. 43, Pt. 2, 124]

Either whip the enemy or get whipped yourself.

> —Union General Philip Sheridan, to General Alfred Torbert, October 9, 1864, Shenandoah Valley campaign
> [CW-3]

We are going to get a twist on those fellows. We are going to lick them out of their boots!

> —Union General Philip Sheridan, to the "retreaters" of his army from Confederate General Jubal Early's attack at Cedar Creek, during Sheridan's "Twelve-Mile Ride," October 19, 1864
> [CW-3]

❖❖❖

God damn you, don't cheer me! If you love your country, come
up to the front! . . . There's lots of fight in you men yet! Come
up, God damn you! Come up!
—Union General Philip Sheridan, to his men, turning the tide of his
army, thus halting a defeat and leading a victory over Confederate
General Jubal Early's army, October 19, 1864
[BCF]

I have the honor to report that my army at Cedar Creek was
attacked this morning before daylight and my left was turned
and driven in confusion; in fact, most of the line was driven in
confusion, with the loss of twenty pieces of artillery. I hastened
from Winchester, where I was on my way from Washington, and
joined the army between Middletown and Newtown, having
been driven back about four miles. I here took the affair in hand
and quickly united the corps, formed a compact line of battle
just in time to repulse an attack of the enemy's, which was hand-
somely done about 1 P.M. At 3 P.M. . . . I attacked with great
vigor, driving and routing the enemy. . . .
—Union General Philip Sheridan, letter to Lt. General Ulysses S.
Grant, from Cedar Creek, Virginia, October 19, 1864
[O.R. 43, Ser 1, Pt. 1, 32]

> Hurrah! Hurrah for Sher-I-dan!
> Hurrah! Hurrah for horse and man! . . .
> I have brought you Sheridan, all the way
> From Winchester, down to save the day.

—"Sheridan's Ride," song by T. Buchanan Read, which dramatized
Sheridan's role in the outcome of the Battle of Cedar Creek and
made his horse Rienzi famous, October 19, 1864. (Rienzi's name
was changed to "Winchester" after the ride.)
[CW-3]

✿

SHERMAN'S MARCH TO THE SEA

After supervising the burning of Atlanta on November 15, Union
Major General William Tecumseh Sherman set off on his three-

hundred-mile-long, sixty-mile-wide march to Savannah, which he captured December 21. For all the destruction of property and foodstuffs, there was relatively little fighting.

I could cut a swath through to the sea, divide the Confederacy in two, and be able to move up in the rear of Lee or do almost anything else that Grant might require of me. Both Jeff Davis, according to the tone of his recent speeches, and Hood want me to fall back. That is the reason I want to go forward.

> —Union Major General William Tecumseh Sherman, to General Horace Porter, September 20, 1864. (Sherman wanted to give up supply lines and bypass Hood's Army of Tennessee.)
> [CG, 293]

I can make this march, and make Georgia howl!

> —Union Major General William Tecumseh Sherman, letter, wherein he continued to try to persuade Lt. General Ulysses S. Grant to allow him to be "turned loose" through Georgia to the coast, October 9, 1864
> [MS-2, 152]

If we can march a well-appointed army right through his territory, it is a demonstration to the world, foreign and domestic, that we have a power which Davis cannot resist. . . . it is overwhelming to my mind that there are thousands of people abroad and in the South who reason thus: If the North can march an army right through the South, it is proof positive that the North can prevail.

> —Union Major General William Tecumseh Sherman, letter to Lt. General Ulysses S. Grant, November 6, 1864
> [CW-3]

Arise for the defense of your native soil! Rally around your patriotic Governor and gallant soldiers! Obstruct and destroy all the roads in Sherman's front, flank, and rear, and his army will soon starve in your midst.

> —Confederate General P. G. T. Beauregard, letter "To the People of Georgia," November 18, 1864
> [MS-2]

❖❖❖

There had been no resistance at that point, nothing to give warning of danger, and the rebels had planted eight-inch shells in the road, with friction-matches to explode them by being trodden on. This was not war, but murder, and it made me very angry.

—Union Major General William Tecumseh Sherman, narrating the March to the Sea, on the young officer whose leg had been blown off and whose horse had been killed by a bomb in the road near Savannah, December 8, 1864. In retaliation Sherman ordered that Confederate prisoners be made to walk ahead of his army; no more mines were found until near Fort McAllister, said Sherman. (The phrase "not war, but murder" and variations on it were made at various times by various generals reminiscing about the war, including by Confederate General D. H. Hill about his division's suicidal attack on Malvern Hill on July 1, 1862: "It was not war—it was murder.")
[MS-2, 194]

Sherman's army is now somewhat in the condition of a ground-mole when he disappears under a lawn. You can here and there trace his track, but you are not quite certain where he will come out until you see his head.

—Union Lt. General Ulysses S. Grant, on Major General William Tecumseh Sherman's army's whereabouts, three weeks after it set out from Atlanta, early December 1864
[CW-3]

> "Hurrah! Hurrah! we bring the jubilee!
> Hurrah! Hurrah! the flag that makes you free!"
> So we sang the chorus from Atlanta to the sea,
> While we were marching through Georgia.

—"Marching Through Georgia," by Henry Clay Work, December 1864
[BG, 581]

The destruction could hardly have been worse, if Atlanta had been a volcano in eruption and the molten lava had flowed in a stream sixty miles wide and five times as long.

—Union soldier, recalling Major General William Tecumseh Sherman's army's March to the Sea
[CW-3]

❖❖❖

This may seem a hard species of warfare, but it brings the sad realities of war home to those who have been directly or indirectly instrumental in involving us in its attendant calamities.

> —Union Major General William Tecumseh Sherman, report at the end of the March to the Sea, about the destruction of property
> [CW-3]

There is no God in war. It is merciless, cruel, vindictive, un-Christian, savage, relentless. It is all that devils could wish for.

> —Union soldier, Sherman's army, reflecting on the March to the Sea across Georgia
> [CW-3]

I beg to present to you as a Christmas-gift the City of Savannah, with one hundred and fifty heavy guns and plenty of ammunition, also about twenty-five thousand bales of cotton.

> —Union Major General William Tecumseh Sherman, telegraph message to President Lincoln, December 22, 1864
> [MS- 2, 231]

I will accept no commission that would tend to create a rivalry with Grant. I want him to hold what he has earned and got. I have all the rank I want. Grant is a great general. I know him well. He stood by me when I was crazy and I stood by him when he was drunk. And now, sir, we stand by each other always.

> —Union Major General William Tecumseh Sherman, letter to his brother, Senator John Sherman of Ohio, on reports that Congress wanted to elevate him to Lt. General and have him share the command of the army with Grant, December 1864
> [CW-3]

❖❖❖

After completing their march through Georgia, Sherman and his army prepared to move up the coast into South Carolina.

Should you capture Charleston, I hope that by some accident the place may be destroyed, and if a little salt should be sown upon its site it may prevent the growth of future crops of nullification and secession.

—Union Major General and Chief of Staff Henry Halleck, letter to Major General William Tecumseh Sherman, December 18, 1864. (Sherman was about to set out on the Carolinas campaign, but rather than Charleston, Sherman headed for Columbia, the capital of South Carolina, which he reached on February 16, 1865.) [MS-2, 223]

The truth is the whole army is burning with an insatiable desire to wreak vengeance upon South Carolina. I almost tremble for her fate, but feel that she deserves all that seems in store for her.

—Union Major General William Tecumseh Sherman, letter to Major General Henry Halleck, December 24, 1864 [MS-2, 227]

✿

BATTLE OF NASHVILLE

The last big battle of the West, part of the Franklin and Nashville campaign, was won by Union General George Thomas's Army of the Cumberland. So frustrated, however, was General in Chief Ulysses S. Grant with what he believed was Thomas's procrastination in Tennessee, that the order for Thomas's removal was on its way to Nashville as Thomas began the attack on December 15. Confederate General John B. Hood led the retreat of his destroyed Army of Tennessee across the Tennessee River on December 26.

If we are to die, let us die like men.

—Confederate General Patrick Cleburne, to an officer as he set out on foot, after two horses were shot from under him, during General J. B. Hood's invasion of Tennessee, November 30, 1864. (Within hours Cleburne was shot dead, near Franklin, Tennessee.) [CW-3]

❖❖❖

I have as much confidence in your conducting a battle rightly as I have in any other officer, but it has seemed to me that you have been slow, and I have had no explanation of affairs to convince me otherwise.

—Union Lt. General Ulysses S. Grant, letter to Major General George Thomas, ordering the attack of the Army of the Cumberland on Hood's Army of Tennessee, December 9, 1864
[CW-3]

Wilson, the Washington authorities treat me as if I was a boy.

—Union Major General George Thomas, in conversation to General James Harrison Wilson, near Nashville, December 10, 1864
[UOF, 102]

I will obey the order as promptly as possible, however much I may regret it, as the attack will have to be made under every disadvantage. The whole country is covered with a perfect sheet of ice and sleet, and it is with difficulty the troops are able to move about on level ground.

—Union Major General George Thomas, letter to Lt. General Ulysses S. Grant, December 11, 1864
[UOF, 91]

Push the enemy now and give him no rest until he is entirely destroyed. . . . Do not stop for trains or supplies, but take them from the country as the enemy has done. Much is now expected.

—Union Lt. General Ulysses S. Grant, letter from Washington, D.C., to Major General George Thomas, December 15, 1864
[USG]

Rally, men, rally! For God's sake, rally! This is the place for brave men to die!

—Confederate General Stephen Lee, to his two divisions, who managed to escape, near Franklin Pike, at the Battle of Nashville, December 15–16, 1864
[CW-3]

❖❖❖

Dang it to hell, Wilson! Didn't I tell you we could lick 'em?
Didn't I tell you we could lick 'em?
    —Union Major General George Thomas to General James Wilson,
    after the victory at the Battle of Nashville, December 16, 1864
    [CW-3]

I doubt if any soldiers in the world ever needed so much cumu-
lative evidence to convince them they were beaten.
    —Union Brigadier General John Schofield, on the 25,000
    Confederate soldiers at Nashville, December 16, 1864. It took
    50,000 Union soldiers two days to defeat them.
    [CW-3]

❊

*The end of the war was coming, but Confederate President
Jefferson Davis insisted on a fight to the finish. So desperate
were the Confederates for troops, that generals and Davis alike
finally agreed on the enlistment of slaves into the army. These
slaves who enlisted, believed Robert E. Lee, should be granted
their freedom. This plan angered many Southerners, who indeed
saw slavery as the Confederacy's raison d'être.*

Our country is ruined if he adopts his suggestion. We give up a
principle when we offer emancipation as a reward or boon, for
we have hitherto contended that slavery was Cuffee's normal
condition, the very best position he could occupy, the one of all
others in which he was happiest, and to take from him that and
give him what we think is misery, is to put ourselves in the
wrong.
    —Catherine Deveraux Edmondston, diary, on seeing a letter from
    Confederate General Robert E. Lee to the Confederate
    Congressional Military Commission, "advising the conscription-
    emancipation and arming of 200,000 slaves immediately," Halifax
    County, North Carolina, December 30, 1864
    [TT]

———————— ❖❖❖ ————————

1865

The war was coming to its last winter and spring. The remaining territory of the Confederacy was starving, but the Confederate Congress's debate over the army's use of slaves as soldiers continued, just as the debate in the U.S. House of Representatives over the merits of the Thirteenth Amendment abolishing slavery continued.

I think that the proposition to make soldiers of our slaves is the most pernicious idea that has been suggested since the war began. It is to me a source of deep mortification and regret to see the name of that good and great man, General R. E. Lee, given as authority for such a policy. . . . The day you make soldiers of them is the beginning of the end of the revolution. If slaves make good soldiers our whole theory of slavery is wrong—but they won't make soldiers.
 —Confederate General Howell Cobb, of Georgia, January 8, 1865
 [O.R. Series 4, Vol. 3, 1009–10]

You will never, never have reliable peace in this country while that institution [of slavery] exists, the perpetual occasion of moral, intellectual, and physical warfare.
 —U.S. Representative John A. Kasson of Iowa, House of Representatives debate on the Thirteenth Amendment, January 10, 1865
 [CWDD, 621]

. . . we must decide whether slavery shall be extinguished by our enemies and the slaves used against us, or use them ourselves at the risk of the effects which may be produced upon our social institutions. My own opinion is that we should employ them without delay. I believe that with proper regulations they can be made efficient soldiers. I think we could at least do as well with them as the enemy. . . . Those who are employed should be freed. It would be neither just nor wise . . . to require them to serve as slaves.

—Confederate General Robert E. Lee, letter to Congressman Andrew Hunter, who sponsored "a Negro soldier bill," January 11, 1865. (The bill did not pass, though Virginia did enact its own law on March 13 to enlist black soldiers—without, however, releasing them from slavery.)
[OR, Ser 4, Vol 3, 1012]

Mr. Speaker, we shall never know why slavery dies so hard in this Republic and in this Hall till we know why sin outlives disaster, and Satan is immortal.

—U.S. Representative James A. Garfield of Ohio, House of Representatives debate on the Thirteenth Amendment, January 12, 1865. (On January 31, the House of Representatives voted in favor of the Thirteenth Amendment. It was ratified by the required two-thirds of the states and put into effect in December. Garfield was elected president in 1880.)
[CWDD, 623]

❖

SHERMAN'S CAROLINAS CAMPAIGN

Sherman led his army north through the swamps of South Carolina and into Columbia, the state's capital, where fire destroyed much of the town. (Columbians blamed the Union soldiers; Sherman blamed the fleeing citizens.) Sherman's army continued on into North Carolina, where in mid-April it finished its 425-mile campaign in Goldsboro.

I think the "poor white trash" of the South are falling out of their ranks by sickness, desertion, and every available means; but there is a large class of vindictive Southerners who will fight to the last. The squabbles in Richmond, the howls in Charleston,

and the disintegration elsewhere, are all good omens for us; we must not relax one iota, but, on the contrary, pile up our efforts.
    —Union Major General William Tecumseh Sherman, letter to Lt. General Ulysses S. Grant at City Point, Virginia, from "In the field, Pocotaligo, South Carolina," January 29, 1865
    [MS-II, 260]

When I learned that Sherman's army was marching through the Salk swamps, making its own corduroy roads at the rate of a dozen miles a day, I made up my mind that there had been no such army in existence since the days of Julius Caesar.
    —Confederate General Joseph Johnston, recalling his feelings on Sherman's Carolinas campaign
    [BCF]

> Hail Columbia, happy land!
> If I don't burn you, I'll be damned.

    —Song of Union General William Tecumseh Sherman's veterans as they marched on Columbia, the capital of South Carolina, February 16, 1865. (Half of the city burned on February 17, though Sherman denied responsibility.)
    [CW-3]

I think the Johnnys are getting rattled; they are afraid of our repeating rifles. They say we are not fair, that we have guns that we load up on Sunday and shoot all the rest of the week. This I know, I feel a good deal more confidence in myself with a 16 shooter in my hands than I used to with a single shot rifle.
    —Union soldier, on the march through the Carolinas under General Sherman, March 1865
    [WSS, 31]

A little more labor, a little more toil on our part, the great race is won, and our Government stands regenerated, after four long years of war.
    —Union Major General William Tecumseh Sherman, "Special Field Orders, No. 54," Smithfield, North Carolina, April 12, 1865
    [MS-II, 344]

❖❖❖

Our late disasters are terrible, but I do not think we should regard them as fatal. I think we can whip the enemy yet, if our people should turn out.

—Confederate President Jefferson Davis, April 12, 1865, to his cabinet and Generals Joseph Johnston and P. G. T. Beauregard, at the temporary capital, Greensboro, North Carolina. Asked his opinion at this point, General Johnston replied, "My views are, sir, that our people are tired of the war, feel themselves whipped, and will not fight." General Beauregard concurred. Nonetheless, Davis continued the war.
[CW-3]

❖

THE END OF THE CONFEDERACY

The outlook was so dim for the Confederacy that in early February intransigent Jefferson Davis allowed three Confederate commissioners, Robert Hunter, Vice President Alexander Stephens, and John Campbell, to go to President Lincoln to see what possibilities existed for negotiating independence for the Confederacy. Lincoln would not bargain on independence, and so Jefferson continued the war.

Mr. President, if we understand you correctly, you think that we of the Confederacy have committed treason; that we are traitors to your government; that we have forfeited our rights, and are proper subjects for the hangman. Is that not about what your words imply?

—Confederate Senator of Virginia Robert Hunter, during peace talks with Abraham Lincoln, aboard the steamer *River Queen*, Hampton Roads, Virginia, February 3, 1865. President Lincoln replied: "Yes. You have stated the proposition better than I did. That is about the size of it."
[CW-3]

Let the sword have no more bloody work to do. If nothing but reunion can be had, let it come, lest a worse fate befall us.

—"Many Soldiers," letter to Confederate President Jefferson Davis, February 5, 1865
[CWT]

❖❖❖

Let us then unite our hands and hearts; lock our shields together, and we may well believe that before another summer solstice falls upon us, it will be the enemy who will be asking us for conferences and occasions in which to make known *our* demands.

> —Confederate President Jefferson Davis, speech at Metropolitan Hall, Richmond, Virginia, February 6, 1865
> [CW-3]

It may seem strange that any men should dare to ask a just God's assistance in wringing their bread from the sweat of other men's faces; but let us judge not, that we be not judged. The prayers of both could not be answered—that of neither has been answered fully. The Almighty has His own purposes.

> —President Abraham Lincoln, Second Inaugural Address, March 4, 1865
> [GS]

That rail-splitting lawyer is one of the wonders of the day. Once at Gettysburg and now again on a greater occasion he has shown a capacity for rising to the demands of the hour which we should not expect from orators or men of the schools. This inaugural strikes me in its grand simplicity and directness as being for all time the keynote of this war; in it a people seemed to speak in the sublimely simple utterance of ruder times.

> —Charles Francis Adams, Jr., letter to his father, the U.S. minister to Great Britain during the war, on President Lincoln's second inaugural speech, March 4, 1865
> [CW-3]

Much benefit is anticipated from this measure, though far less than would have resulted from its adoption at an earlier date, so as to afford time for organization and instruction during the winter months.

> —Confederate President Jefferson Davis, March 13, 1865, signing a bill that would permit enlisting slaves into the Confederate army
> [CW-3]

❖❖❖

If we are right in passing this measure, we were wrong in deny-
ing the old government the right to interfere with the institution
of slavery and to emancipate slaves.

> —Confederate Senator Robert Hunter, March 13, 1865, on the bill
> that would allow enlisting African-Americans into the Confederate
> army
> [CW-3]

General Sheridan, when this peculiar war began I thought a cav-
alryman should be at least six feet four inches high, but I have
changed my mind. Five feet four will do in a pinch.

> —President Abraham Lincoln, speaking to General Philip
> Sheridan, after his successful cavalry raid in northern Virginia,
> March 26, 1865
> [CW-3]

My God, my God! Can't you spare more effusions of blood? We
have had so much of it.

> —President Abraham Lincoln in conversation with Generals Grant
> and Sherman, on board the *River Queen*, when they told the presi-
> dent that Confederate General in Chief Robert E. Lee might have
> the Army of Northern Virginia fight one last battle, March 28, 1865
> [CW-3]

He is at rest now, and we who are left are the ones to suffer.

> —Confederate General Robert E. Lee on the death of General
> A. P. Hill, killed in the final defense of Petersburg, Virginia, April 2,
> 1865
> [CW-3]

Let us not then despond, my countrymen, but, relying on the
never-failing mercies and protecting care of our God, let us
meet the foe with fresh defiance, with unconquered and uncon-
querable hearts.

> —Confederate President Jefferson Davis, proclamation, "To the
> People of the Confederate States of America," April 4, 1865
> [CW-3]

Your General lives. My Colonel lives. What words can express our gratitude? What is the loss of home and good compared with the loss of our own flesh and blood? Alas! Alas! for those who have lost all!

—"Agnes," letter to Sara Agnes Porter, on the entry of Union troops to Richmond, Virginia, April 5, 1865
[CWT]

Thank God I have lived to see this. It seems to me that I have been dreaming a horrid dream for four years, and now the nightmare is gone.

—President Abraham Lincoln to Admiral David Porter, at the Union base on the James River, April 3, 1865
[BCF]

When you ask me what *I* would do, my reply is—I would arrest them, I would try them, I would convict them, and I would hang them. . . . Treason must be made odious; traitors must be punished and impoverished.

—Vice President Andrew Johnson, speech on the Confederate leaders, Washington, D.C., early April 1865. (After becoming president shortly thereafter, however, Johnson tried to honor Lincoln's conciliatory policy.)
[CW-3]

Sheridan says, "If the thing be pressed I think that Lee will surrender." Let the *thing* be pressed.

—President Abraham Lincoln, letter to Lt. General Ulysses S. Grant, April 7, 1865
[CW-3]

I have a great mind to summon Lee to surrender.

—Union Lt. General Ulysses S. Grant, to Generals Edward Ord and John Gibbon, April 7, 1865. (Grant immediately composed a letter to Confederate General Robert E. Lee, in which he stated: "The results of the last week must convince you of the hopelessness of further resistance on the part of the Army of Northern Virginia in this struggle. I feel that it is so, and regard it as my duty to shift from myself the responsibility of any further effusion of blood by asking of you the surrender of that portion of the C.S. Army known as the Army of Northern Virginia.")
[CW-3]

———————❖❖❖———————

Then there is nothing left for me to do but go and see General Grant, and I would rather die a thousand deaths.

> —Confederate General Robert E. Lee to his staff, Appomattox Courthouse, Virginia, April 9, 1865
> [CW-3]

I felt like anything rather than rejoicing at the downfall of a foe who had fought so long and valiantly, and had suffered so much for a cause, though that cause was, I believe, one of the worst for which a people ever fought.

> —Union Lt. General Ulysses S. Grant, reflecting in his *Memoirs* on Confederate General Robert E. Lee's surrender, Appomattox Courthouse, Virginia, April 9, 1865
> [USG]

The war is over. The rebels are our countrymen again.

> —Union Lt. General Ulysses S. Grant to his staff, April 9, 1865
> [CW-3]

Men, we have fought the war together, and I have done the best I could for you. You will all be paroled and go to your homes until exchanged.

> —Confederate General Robert E. Lee, after being asked by his troops, "General, are we surrendered?" April 9, 1865. (Another soldier quoted Lee this way: "Men, we have fought through the war together. I have done the best that I could for you. My heart is too full to say more.")
> [CW-3; WW]

With an unceasing admiration of your constancy and devotion to your Country, and a grateful remembrance of your kind and generous consideration for myself, I bid you all an affectionate farewell.

> —Confederate General Robert E. Lee, closing of General Orders No. 9, Headquarters of the Army of Northern Virginia, April 10, 1865
> [CW-3]

———————❖❖❖———————

I am sorry the war is ended. Pray do not think me murderous. No; but all the punishment we could inflict on the rebels would not atone for one drop of blood so cruelly spilled. I would exterminate them root and branch. They have often said they preferred it before subjugation, and, with the help of God, I would give it them.

—Union soldier T. R. Keenan, after Lee's surrender
[Wiley, *Billy Yank*: ref: Lydia Minturn Post, editor, *Soldiers' Letters*, 468–469]

The evacuation of Petersburg and Richmond, and the surrender of the principal insurgent army, give hope of a righteous and speedy peace whose joyous expression can not be restrained.

—President Abraham Lincoln, speech from a White House balcony, April 11, 1865

Now, by God, I'll put him through. That is the last speech he will ever make.

—John Wilkes Booth, on President Lincoln's reconstruction speech, April 11, 1865. (It was in fact Lincoln's last speech. Booth, an actor, and his conspirators soon carried out the president's assassination.)
[BCF]

*

THE ASSASSINATION

Abraham Lincoln, 56 years old, the 16th president of the United States, relieved by the surrender of Lee's Army of Northern Virginia, with the war's end and the country's reunion in sight, was shot in the head by an actor, John Wilkes Booth, during a play at Ford's Theatre in Washington, D.C., on April 14, 1865. He died the next morning.

Shoo; scare them off. Enough lives have been sacrificed.

—President Abraham Lincoln, to his cabinet, on what legal sanctions to take with the Confederacy leaders, April 13, 1865
[CW-3]

❖❖❖

Creswell, old fellow, everything is bright this morning. The war is over. It has been a tough time, but we have lived it out. Or some of us have.

 —President Abraham Lincoln to Senator John Creswell of Maryland, April 14, 1865
[CW-3]

We must both be more cheerful in the future. Between the war and the loss of our darling Willie, we have both been very miserable.

 —President Abraham Lincoln to Mary, his wife, April 14, 1865. (One of their young sons had died of disease in 1863. On this night the Lincolns went to the theater.)
[CW-3]

Sic semper tyrannis! The South is avenged!

 —John Wilkes Booth, announcing on stage at Ford's Theatre, Washington, D.C., after shooting President Lincoln, April 14, 1865. (The Latin words mean: "Thus always to tyrants!") After his escape from Washington, D.C., Wilkes was tracked down and killed on April 26, and his conspirators (other officials were to be assassinated, and Secretary of State William Seward was stabbed, but not killed) were convicted and executed or sentenced in July 1865.
[CWDD, 676; Boatner]

His wound is mortal. It is impossible for him to recover.

 —Charles A. Leale, assistant surgeon of the U.S. Volunteers, the first doctor to arrive at Lincoln's box in Ford's Theatre, Washington, D.C., after the actor John Wilkes Booth shot the president, April 14, 1865. Lincoln died the morning of April 15.
[CW-3]

Now he belongs to the ages.

 —Secretary of War Edwin Stanton, at Lincoln's bedside as the president died, April 15, 1865
[CW-3]

The only assurance I can now give of the future is reference to the past. Toil, and an honest advocacy of the great principles of

free government, have been my lot. The duties have been mine; the consequences are God's.
> —President Andrew Johnson, speech to cabinet and senators, April 15, 1865, Washington, D.C., having taken the oath of office as the 17th president of the United States
> [CW-3]

Lincoln's death—black, black, black—as you look toward the sky—long broad black like great serpents slowly undulating in every direction—New York is distinguished for its countless gay flags—every house seems to have a flag staff—on all these the colors were at half mast.
> —Walt Whitman, diary, April 15, 1865
> [WWCW]

> Thy task is done; the bound are free:
> We bear thee to an honored grave,
> Whose proudest monument shall be
> The broken fetters of the slave.
> —William Cullen Bryant, poem, "Abraham Lincoln"
> [CWP]

I knowed when he went away he wasn't ever coming back.
> —Sally Bush Lincoln, President Lincoln's stepmother, 1865. (Abraham Lincoln was buried in Springfield, Illinois, on May 4, 1865.)
> [CW-3]

Certainly I have no special regard for Mr. Lincoln, but there are a great many men of whose end I would rather hear than his. I fear it will be disastrous to our people, and I regret it deeply.
> —Confederate President Jefferson Davis, hearing of President Lincoln's assassination, April 19, 1865
> [CW-3]

I know this foul murder will bring down worse miseries on us.
> —Mary Boykin Chesnut, diary, Chester, South Carolina, upon hearing of President Lincoln's assassination, April 22, 1865
> [WW]

❖❖❖

SURRENDER

The Confederate government evacuated Richmond on April 2, and reorganized in Danville, Virginia, on April 4, before fleeing on April 10 to North Carolina. After Davis authorized Confederate General Joseph Johnston's negotiations for the surrender of the Army of Tennessee, which was completed on April 26, Davis attempted to escape, but was captured on May 10.

On this solemn and joyful day we again lift to the breeze our father's flag, now again the banner of the United States, with the fervent prayer that God would crown it with honor, protect it from treason, and send it down to our children with all the blessings of civilization, liberty, and religion. . . . Ruin sits in the cradle of treason, rebellion has perished, but there flies the same flag that was insulted! With starry eyes it looks all over this bay for that banner that supplanted it, and sees it not.
—Reverend Henry Ward Beecher, speech, Fort Sumter, Charleston Harbor, South Carolina, April 14, 1865
[UR]

> John Brown's body lies a-mould'ring in the grave,
> John Brown's body lies a-mould'ring in the grave,
> John Brown's body lies a-mould'ring in the grave,
> His soul is marching on.
>
> Glory! Glory Hallelujah!
> Glory! Glory Hallelujah!
> Glory! Glory Hallelujah!
> His soul is marching on.
>
> They'll hang Jeff Davis on a sour apple tree,
> As they go marching on.

—"John Brown's Body," words by Thomas B. Bishop, played at Fort Sumter, April 14, 1865
[BG, 564]

❖❖❖

The South is broken and ruined and appeals to our pity. To ride the people down with persecutions and military exactions would be like slashing away at the crew of a sinking ship.

—Union Major General William Tecumseh Sherman, speaking to General John A. Rawlins, April 1865
[CW-3]

See here, gentlemen. Who is doing this surrendering anyhow? If this thing goes on, you'll have me sending a letter of apology to Jeff Davis.

—Union Major General William Tecumseh Sherman, to Confederate General Joseph Johnston and Secretary of War John Breckinridge, while negotiating a "Memorandum, or Basis of Agreement" on the surrender of Johnston's Army of Tennessee, April 18, 1865
[CW-3]

One hundred thousand dollars reward in gold, will be paid to any person or persons who will apprehend and deliver Jefferson Davis to any of the military authorities of the United States. Several million of specie, reported to be with him, will become the property of the captors.

—Union General James H. Wilson, order, May 6, 1865. (Davis was captured May 10, in Irwinsville, Georgia.)
[CR]

I have never on the field of battle sent you where I was unwilling to go myself, nor would I now advise you to a course which I felt myself unwilling to pursue. You have been good soldiers, you can be good citizens. Obey the laws, preserve your honor, and the government to which you have surrendered can afford to be and will be magnanimous.

—Confederate Lt. General Nathan Bedford Forrest, farewell address to his men, Gainesville, May 9, 1865
[CW-3]

❖❖❖

The war is over; the South is conquered; I have no longer any country but America, and it is for the honor of America, as for my own honor and life, that I plead against this degradation. Kill me! Kill me, rather than inflict on me, and on my people through me, this insult worse than death.

—Jefferson Davis, protesting being shackled at Fort Monroe, Virginia, May 23, 1865. (His shackles were soon removed, but he remained imprisoned until 1867.)

[CWT: ref: *Prison Life of Jefferson Davis*, 1867]

Post-War

Andrew Johnson, of Tennessee, the president after Lincoln's assassination, announced on May 10 that "armed resistance to the authority of this Government in the said insurrectionary States may be regarded as virtually at an end." (The last major Confederate army to surrender was General E. Kirby Smith's Trans-Mississippi Department, on May 26. One Confederate ship continued to plunder until December 1865, when it finally learned of the surrender.) On May 29 President Johnson issued an amnesty proclamation for most of those who fought for the Confederacy. Though Johnson as governor of Tennessee and then as vice president had advocated punitive measures against the seceding states, his Reconstruction policies for the most part tried to honor Abraham Lincoln's more generous intentions.

Jefferson Davis was released from imprisonment in Fort Monroe, Virginia, in 1867, and lived until 1881, writing his memoirs. Robert E. Lee, having served after the war as president of Washington University (now Washington and Lee University), died in 1870. Ulysses S. Grant succeeded Andrew Johnson as president and served two terms, but his administration was riddled with graft and he was unhappy with the job. He died in 1885, only just managing to finish his great Personal Memoirs of U. S. Grant, *which focused primarily on the Civil War.*

If this was a civil war, I hope never to fight in an uncivil one!
—Confederate Major Charles H. Smith, of Georgia, also known as "Bill Arp," a weekly newspaper columnist
[TT]

I am a good old Rebel,
And that's just what I am;
And for this land of freedom,
I do not care a damn,
I'm glad I fit agin it,
I only wish I'd won;
And I didn't ax no pardoning
For anything I done.
—"Lay of the Last Rebel," song by Major Innes Randolph
[CWT]

Two dead men have killed slavery. What John Brown's death had initiated, Lincoln's death brought to completion.
—Victor Hugo, French author, notebook, September–October 1865
[ELCW, 306]

Neither slavery nor involuntary servitude, except as a punishment for crime whereof the party shall have been duly convicted, shall exist within the United States, or any place subject to their jurisdiction.
—Thirteenth Amendment to the Constitution of the United States, December 18, 1865

For the present, and so long as there are living witnesses of the great war of sections, there will be people who will not be consoled for the loss of a cause which they believed to be holy. As time passes, people, even of the South, will begin to wonder how it was possible that their ancestors ever fought for or justified institutions which acknowledged the right of property in man.
—Ulysses S. Grant, *The Personal Memoirs of U. S. Grant*, 1885
[USG]

❖❖❖

Sources

Note: Each source has a lettered code in square brackets that corresponds to the quotations in this book.

Adams, George W. *Doctors in Blue.* Dayton, Ohio: Morningside Publishers, 1985. [DB]

Adams, Henry. *The Education of Henry Adams.* Boston: Houghton-Mifflin, 1918. [EHA]

Alcott, Louisa May. *Hospital Sketches.* Boston: Applewood Books, 1986. [HS]

Arnold, Thomas Jackson. *Early Life and Letters of Gen. Thomas J. (Stonewall) Jackson.* New York: Fleming H. Revell, 1916. [ELLTJJ]

Ayers, Edward L. *"A House Divided . . .": A Century of Great Civil War Quotations.* New York: John Wiley & Sons, 1997. [AHD]

Bartlett, Asa W. *History of the Twelfth Regiment New Hampshire Volunteers.* Concord, N.H.: Ira Evans, 1897. [NHV]

Boatner, Mark Mayo. *Civil War Dictionary.* New York: David McKay Co., 1959. [CWD]

Bollet, Alfred. *Civil War Medicine: Challenges and Triumphs.* Tucson, Ariz.: Galen Press, 2002. [CWM]

Botkin, B. A. *A Civil War Treasury.* New York: Random House, 1960. [CWT]

Brockett, Linus P., and Mary C. Vaughan. *Women's Work in the Civil War.* Philadelphia: Hubbard Brothers, 1888. [BV]

Brown, William Wells. *The Black Man: His Antecedents, His Genius, and His Achievements.* New York: T. Hamilton, 1863. [BM]

Catton, Bruce. *The Coming Fury.* New York: Doubleday, 1972. [CF]

Catton, Bruce. *Never Call Retreat.* New York: Doubleday, 1965. [NCR]

Chesnut, Mary. *A Diary from Dixie.* New York: Appleton & Co., ca. 1905. [CCW]

Commager, Henry Steele. *The Blue and the Gray: The Story of the Civil War as Told by Participants.* Indianapolis: Bobbs-Merrill, 1950. [BG]

Denney, Robert E. *The Civil War Years:A Day-by-Day Chronicle of the Life of a Nation.* New York: Sterling Publishing, 1994. [CWY]

Douglass' Monthly [periodical]. 1861–1862. [DM]

Fehrenbacher, Don E. and Virginia Fehrenbacher. *Recollected Words of Abraham Lincoln.* Stanford, Calif.: Stanford University Press, 1996. [RWAL]

Foote, Shelby. *The Civil War: A Narrative.* 3 vols. New York: Random House. [CW-1, -2, -3]

Ford, Worthington Chauncey. *A Cycle of Adams Letters.* Vol. I. Boston: Houghton-Mifflin, 1920. [CAL]

Freeman, Douglas Southall. *Lee's Lieutenants: A Study in Command.* Vol. 1. New York: Scribner's, 1942. [LL]

Glicksberg, Charles, ed. *Walt Whitman and the Civil War.* New York: A. S. Barnes, 1963. [WWCW]

Grant, Ulysses S. *The Personal Memoirs of U. S. Grant.* New York: Da Capo, 1952. [USG]

Harwell, Richard B. *The Confederate Reader: As the South Saw the War.* New York: Dover, 1989. [CR]

Harwell, Richard B. *The Union Reader: As the North Saw the War.* New York: Dover, 1996. [UR]

Hay, John. *Lincoln and the Civil War in the Diaries and Letters of John Hay.* New York: Dodd, Mead & Co., 1939. [LCW]

Holmes, Oliver Wendell, Jr. *Touched with Fire: Civil War Letters and Diary of Oliver Wendell Holmes, Jr.: 1861–1864.* New York: Da Capo, 1969. [OWH]

Holzer, Harold. *Witness to War: The Civil War, 1861–1865.* New York: Perigee, 1996. [WW]

Jackson, Mary Anna. *Life and Letters of General Thomas J. Jackson.* New York: Harper, 1892. [TJJ]

Lee, Robert E. *Wartime Papers of Robert E. Lee.* New York: Da Capo, 1961. [REL]

———————— ❖❖❖ ————————

Lincoln, Abraham. (John Grafton, editor). *Great Speeches*. Mineola, N.Y.: Dover, 1991. [GS]

Livermore, Thomas L. *Days and Events*. Boston: Houghton-Mifflin, 1920. [DE]

Long, E. B., with Barbara Long. *The Civil War Day by Day: An Almanac: 1861–1865*. Garden City, N.Y.: Doubleday, 1971. [CWDD]

McClellan, George B. *McClellan's Own Story: The War for the Union*. New York: Webster, 1887. [MOS]

McClure, Alexander. *Abraham Lincoln and Men of War-Times*. Philadelphia: Times Publishing, 1892. [AC]

McCormick, A. A. *Modern Eloquence*. Vol. 10. Philadelphia: J. D. Morris, 1901. [ME]

McPherson, James M. *The Battle Cry of Freedom: The Civil War Era*. New York: Ballantine, 1989. [BCF]

McPherson, James M. *What They Fought For: 1861–1865*. New York: Anchor, 1995. [WTFF]

Moore, Frank, editor. *The Rebellion Record: A Diary of American Events*. 10 vols. New York: Putnam, also, repr. later, D. Van Nostrand, 1861–1867. [RR-1, -2, etc., with sections: Diary, Documents, Poetry]

Negri, Paul. *Civil War Poetry: An Anthology*. Mineola, N.Y.: Dover, 1997. [CWP]

Nevins, Alan. *The Emergence of Lincoln*. Vol. II. New York: Scribner, 1950. [EL]

Nichols, C. *Life of Abraham Lincoln*. New York: Mast, Crowell & Kirkpatrick, 1896. [LAL]

Norton, O. W. *Army Letters: 1861–1865*. Chicago: O. L. Deming, 1903. [OWN]

Poe, Clarence. *True Tales of the South at War*. Mineola, N.Y.: Dover, 1995. [TT]

Pollard, Edward A. *The Southern History of the War*. New York: C. B. Richardson, 1866. [SHW]

Porter, Horace. *Campaigning with Grant*. New York: The Century Co., 1897. [CG]

Sears, Steven W. *Chancellorsville*. Boston: Houghton-Mifflin, 1996. [SS]

Sherman, William Tecumseh. *Home Letters of General Sherman*. New York: Scribner, 1909. [HLGS]

❖❖❖

Sherman, William Tecumseh. *The Memoirs of General William T. Sherman.* 2 vols. New York: Appleton & Co., 1875. [MS-1, MS-2]

Sideman, Belle Becker. *Europe Looks at the Civil War.* New York: Orion Press, 1960. [ELCW]

Stoddard, William. *Inside the White House in War Times.* New York: Webster, 1890. [IWH]

Strong, George Templeton. *Diary of the Civil War.* New York: Macmillan, 1962. [GTS]

Trollope, Anthony. *North America.* Philadelphia: J. B. Lippincott, 1862. [NA]

Upson, Thomas F. *With Sherman to the Sea.* Baton Rouge: Louisiana State University Press, 1943. [WSS]

Villard, Oswald Garrison. *John Brown: A Biography: 1800–1859.* Garden City, N.Y.: Doubleday, Doran & Co., 1929. [JB]

Wakelyn, Jon L. *Southern Pamphlets on Secession: November 1860–April 1861.* Chapel Hill, N.C.: University of North Carolina Press, 1996. [SPS]

War of the Rebellion: A Compilation of the Official Records of the Union and Confederate Armies. Washington, D.C.: Government Printing Office, 1880. [OR]

Watkins, Sam R. *1861–1862: "Co. Aytch."* Nashville: Cumberland Presbyterian Publishing House, 1882. [SRW]

Whitman, Walt. *Civil War Poetry and Prose.* Mineola, N.Y.: Dover, 1995. [CWPP]

Wiley, Bell Irvin. *The Life of Billy Yank.* Indianapolis: Bobbs-Merrill, 1952. [BY]

Wiley, Bell Irvin. *The Life of Johnny Reb.* Indianapolis: Bobbs-Merrill, 1943. [JR]

Wilson, James Harrison. *Under the Old Flag.* Vol. 2. New York: Appleton & Co., 1912. [UOF]

Web Sources

Sullivan Ballou: http://www.pbs.org/civilwar/war/ballou_letter.html

General Reynolds, first quote at Gettysburg:
http://www.civilweek.com/1863/jul0163Sup.htm

Index of Authors

❖❖❖

❖❖❖

A CATALOG OF SELECTED
DOVER BOOKS
IN ALL FIELDS OF INTEREST

A CATALOG OF SELECTED DOVER
BOOKS IN ALL FIELDS OF INTEREST

CONCERNING THE SPIRITUAL IN ART, Wassily Kandinsky. Pioneering work by father of abstract art. Thoughts on color theory, nature of art. Analysis of earlier masters. 12 illustrations. 80pp. of text. 5⅜ x 8½. 23411-8

ANIMALS: 1,419 Copyright-Free Illustrations of Mammals, Birds, Fish, Insects, etc., Jim Harter (ed.). Clear wood engravings present, in extremely lifelike poses, over 1,000 species of animals. One of the most extensive pictorial sourcebooks of its kind. Captions. Index. 284pp. 9 x 12. 23766-4

CELTIC ART: The Methods of Construction, George Bain. Simple geometric techniques for making Celtic interlacements, spirals, Kells-type initials, animals, humans, etc. Over 500 illustrations. 160pp. 9 x 12. (Available in U.S. only.) 22923-8

AN ATLAS OF ANATOMY FOR ARTISTS, Fritz Schider. Most thorough reference work on art anatomy in the world. Hundreds of illustrations, including selections from works by Vesalius, Leonardo, Goya, Ingres, Michelangelo, others. 593 illustrations. 192pp. 7⅛ x 10¼. 20241-0

CELTIC HAND STROKE-BY-STROKE (Irish Half-Uncial from "The Book of Kells"): An Arthur Baker Calligraphy Manual, Arthur Baker. Complete guide to creating each letter of the alphabet in distinctive Celtic manner. Covers hand position, strokes, pens, inks, paper, more. Illustrated. 48pp. 8¼ x 11. 24336-2

EASY ORIGAMI, John Montroll. Charming collection of 32 projects (hat, cup, pelican, piano, swan, many more) specially designed for the novice origami hobbyist. Clearly illustrated easy-to-follow instructions insure that even beginning papercrafters will achieve successful results. 48pp. 8¼ x 11. 27298-2

THE COMPLETE BOOK OF BIRDHOUSE CONSTRUCTION FOR WOODWORKERS, Scott D. Campbell. Detailed instructions, illustrations, tables. Also data on bird habitat and instinct patterns. Bibliography. 3 tables. 63 illustrations in 15 figures. 48pp. 5¼ x 8½. 24407-5

BLOOMINGDALE'S ILLUSTRATED 1886 CATALOG: Fashions, Dry Goods and Housewares, Bloomingdale Brothers. Famed merchants' extremely rare catalog depicting about 1,700 products: clothing, housewares, firearms, dry goods, jewelry, more. Invaluable for dating, identifying vintage items. Also, copyright-free graphics for artists, designers. Co-published with Henry Ford Museum & Greenfield Village. 160pp. 8¼ x 11. 25780-0

HISTORIC COSTUME IN PICTURES, Braun & Schneider. Over 1,450 costumed figures in clearly detailed engravings–from dawn of civilization to end of 19th century. Captions. Many folk costumes. 256pp. 8⅜ x 11¾. 23150-X

STICKLEY CRAFTSMAN FURNITURE CATALOGS, Gustav Stickley and L. & J. G. Stickley. Beautiful, functional furniture in two authentic catalogs from 1910. 594 illustrations, including 277 photos, show settles, rockers, armchairs, reclining chairs, bookcases, desks, tables. 183pp. 6½ x 9¼. 23838-5

AMERICAN LOCOMOTIVES IN HISTORIC PHOTOGRAPHS: 1858 to 1949, Ron Ziel (ed.). A rare collection of 126 meticulously detailed official photographs, called "builder portraits," of American locomotives that majestically chronicle the rise of steam locomotive power in America. Introduction. Detailed captions. xi+ 129pp. 9 x 12. 27393-8

AMERICA'S LIGHTHOUSES: An Illustrated History, Francis Ross Holland, Jr. Delightfully written, profusely illustrated fact-filled survey of over 200 American lighthouses since 1716. History, anecdotes, technological advances, more. 240pp. 8 x 10¾. 25576-X

TOWARDS A NEW ARCHITECTURE, Le Corbusier. Pioneering manifesto by founder of "International School." Technical and aesthetic theories, views of industry, economics, relation of form to function, "mass-production split" and much more. Profusely illustrated. 320pp. 6⅛ x 9¼. (Available in U.S. only.) 25023-7

HOW THE OTHER HALF LIVES, Jacob Riis. Famous journalistic record, exposing poverty and degradation of New York slums around 1900, by major social reformer. 100 striking and influential photographs. 233pp. 10 x 7⅞. 22012-5

FRUIT KEY AND TWIG KEY TO TREES AND SHRUBS, William M. Harlow. One of the handiest and most widely used identification aids. Fruit key covers 120 deciduous and evergreen species; twig key 160 deciduous species. Easily used. Over 300 photographs. 126pp. 5⅜ x 8½. 20511-8

COMMON BIRD SONGS, Dr. Donald J. Borror. Songs of 60 most common U.S. birds: robins, sparrows, cardinals, bluejays, finches, more–arranged in order of increasing complexity. Up to 9 variations of songs of each species.

Cassette and manual 99911-4

ORCHIDS AS HOUSE PLANTS, Rebecca Tyson Northen. Grow cattleyas and many other kinds of orchids–in a window, in a case, or under artificial light. 63 illustrations. 148pp. 5⅜ x 8½. 23261-1

MONSTER MAZES, Dave Phillips. Masterful mazes at four levels of difficulty. Avoid deadly perils and evil creatures to find magical treasures. Solutions for all 32 exciting illustrated puzzles. 48pp. 8¼ x 11. 26005-4

MOZART'S DON GIOVANNI (DOVER OPERA LIBRETTO SERIES), Wolfgang Amadeus Mozart. Introduced and translated by Ellen H. Bleiler. Standard Italian libretto, with complete English translation. Convenient and thoroughly portable–an ideal companion for reading along with a recording or the performance itself. Introduction. List of characters. Plot summary. 121pp. 5¼ x 8½. 24944-1

TECHNICAL MANUAL AND DICTIONARY OF CLASSICAL BALLET, Gail Grant. Defines, explains, comments on steps, movements, poses and concepts. 15-page pictorial section. Basic book for student, viewer. 127pp. 5⅜ x 8½. 21843-0

THE CLARINET AND CLARINET PLAYING, David Pino. Lively, comprehensive work features suggestions about technique, musicianship, and musical interpretation, as well as guidelines for teaching, making your own reeds, and preparing for public performance. Includes an intriguing look at clarinet history. "A godsend," *The Clarinet,* Journal of the International Clarinet Society. Appendixes. 7 illus. 320pp. 5⅜ x 8½. 40270-3

HOLLYWOOD GLAMOR PORTRAITS, John Kobal (ed.). 145 photos from 1926-49. Harlow, Gable, Bogart, Bacall; 94 stars in all. Full background on photographers, technical aspects. 160pp. 8⅜ x 11¼. 23352-9

THE ANNOTATED CASEY AT THE BAT: A Collection of Ballads about the Mighty Casey/Third, Revised Edition, Martin Gardner (ed.). Amusing sequels and parodies of one of America's best-loved poems: Casey's Revenge, Why Casey Whiffed, Casey's Sister at the Bat, others. 256pp. 5⅜ x 8½. 28598-7

THE RAVEN AND OTHER FAVORITE POEMS, Edgar Allan Poe. Over 40 of the author's most memorable poems: "The Bells," "Ulalume," "Israfel," "To Helen," "The Conqueror Worm," "Eldorado," "Annabel Lee," many more. Alphabetic lists of titles and first lines. 64pp. 5$\frac{3}{16}$ x 8¼. 26685-0

PERSONAL MEMOIRS OF U. S. GRANT, Ulysses Simpson Grant. Intelligent, deeply moving firsthand account of Civil War campaigns, considered by many the finest military memoirs ever written. Includes letters, historic photographs, maps and more. 528pp. 6⅛ x 9¼. 28587-1

ANCIENT EGYPTIAN MATERIALS AND INDUSTRIES, A. Lucas and J. Harris. Fascinating, comprehensive, thoroughly documented text describes this ancient civilization's vast resources and the processes that incorporated them in daily life, including the use of animal products, building materials, cosmetics, perfumes and incense, fibers, glazed ware, glass and its manufacture, materials used in the mummification process, and much more. 544pp. 6⅛ x 9¼. (Available in U.S. only.) 40446-3

RUSSIAN STORIES/RUSSKIE RASSKAZY: A Dual-Language Book, edited by Gleb Struve. Twelve tales by such masters as Chekhov, Tolstoy, Dostoevsky, Pushkin, others. Excellent word-for-word English translations on facing pages, plus teaching and study aids, Russian/English vocabulary, biographical/critical introductions, more. 416pp. 5⅜ x 8½. 26244-8

PHILADELPHIA THEN AND NOW: 60 Sites Photographed in the Past and Present, Kenneth Finkel and Susan Oyama. Rare photographs of City Hall, Logan Square, Independence Hall, Betsy Ross House, other landmarks juxtaposed with contemporary views. Captures changing face of historic city. Introduction. Captions. 128pp. 8¼ x 11. 25790-8

AIA ARCHITECTURAL GUIDE TO NASSAU AND SUFFOLK COUNTIES, LONG ISLAND, The American Institute of Architects, Long Island Chapter, and the Society for the Preservation of Long Island Antiquities. Comprehensive, well-researched and generously illustrated volume brings to life over three centuries of Long Island's great architectural heritage. More than 240 photographs with authoritative, extensively detailed captions. 176pp. 8¼ x 11. 26946-9

NORTH AMERICAN INDIAN LIFE: Customs and Traditions of 23 Tribes, Elsie Clews Parsons (ed.). 27 fictionalized essays by noted anthropologists examine religion, customs, government, additional facets of life among the Winnebago, Crow, Zuni, Eskimo, other tribes. 480pp. 6⅛ x 9¼. 27377-6

FRANK LLOYD WRIGHT'S DANA HOUSE, Donald Hoffmann. Pictorial essay of residential masterpiece with over 160 interior and exterior photos, plans, elevations, sketches and studies. 128pp. 9¼ x 10¾. 29120-0

THE MALE AND FEMALE FIGURE IN MOTION: 60 Classic Photographic Sequences, Eadweard Muybridge. 60 true-action photographs of men and women walking, running, climbing, bending, turning, etc., reproduced from rare 19th-century masterpiece. vi + 121pp. 9 x 12. 24745-7

1001 QUESTIONS ANSWERED ABOUT THE SEASHORE, N. J. Berrill and Jacquelyn Berrill. Queries answered about dolphins, sea snails, sponges, starfish, fishes, shore birds, many others. Covers appearance, breeding, growth, feeding, much more. 305pp. 5¼ x 8¼. 23366-9

ATTRACTING BIRDS TO YOUR YARD, William J. Weber. Easy-to-follow guide offers advice on how to attract the greatest diversity of birds: birdhouses, feeders, water and waterers, much more. 96pp. 5³⁄₁₆ x 8¼. 28927-3

MEDICINAL AND OTHER USES OF NORTH AMERICAN PLANTS: A Historical Survey with Special Reference to the Eastern Indian Tribes, Charlotte Erichsen-Brown. Chronological historical citations document 500 years of usage of plants, trees, shrubs native to eastern Canada, northeastern U.S. Also complete identifying information. 343 illustrations. 544pp. 6½ x 9¼. 25951-X

STORYBOOK MAZES, Dave Phillips. 23 stories and mazes on two-page spreads: Wizard of Oz, Treasure Island, Robin Hood, etc. Solutions. 64pp. 8¼ x 11. 23628-5

AMERICAN NEGRO SONGS: 230 Folk Songs and Spirituals, Religious and Secular, John W. Work. This authoritative study traces the African influences of songs sung and played by black Americans at work, in church, and as entertainment. The author discusses the lyric significance of such songs as "Swing Low, Sweet Chariot," "John Henry," and others and offers the words and music for 230 songs. Bibliography. Index of Song Titles. 272pp. 6½ x 9¼. 40271-1

MOVIE-STAR PORTRAITS OF THE FORTIES, John Kobal (ed.). 163 glamor, studio photos of 106 stars of the 1940s: Rita Hayworth, Ava Gardner, Marlon Brando, Clark Gable, many more. 176pp. 8⅜ x 11¼. 23546-7

BENCHLEY LOST AND FOUND, Robert Benchley. Finest humor from early 30s, about pet peeves, child psychologists, post office and others. Mostly unavailable elsewhere. 73 illustrations by Peter Arno and others. 183pp. 5⅜ x 8½. 22410-4

YEKL and THE IMPORTED BRIDEGROOM AND OTHER STORIES OF YIDDISH NEW YORK, Abraham Cahan. Film Hester Street based on *Yekl* (1896). Novel, other stories among first about Jewish immigrants on N.Y.'s East Side. 240pp. 5⅜ x 8½. 22427-9

SELECTED POEMS, Walt Whitman. Generous sampling from *Leaves of Grass*. Twenty-four poems include "I Hear America Singing," "Song of the Open Road," "I Sing the Body Electric," "When Lilacs Last in the Dooryard Bloom'd," "O Captain! My Captain!"—all reprinted from an authoritative edition. Lists of titles and first lines. 128pp. 5³⁄₁₆ x 8¼. 26878-0

THE BEST TALES OF HOFFMANN, E. T. A. Hoffmann. 10 of Hoffmann's most important stories: "Nutcracker and the King of Mice," "The Golden Flowerpot," etc. 458pp. 5⅜ x 8½. 21793-0

FROM FETISH TO GOD IN ANCIENT EGYPT, E. A. Wallis Budge. Rich detailed survey of Egyptian conception of "God" and gods, magic, cult of animals, Osiris, more. Also, superb English translations of hymns and legends. 240 illustrations. 545pp. 5⅜ x 8½. 25803-3

FRENCH STORIES/CONTES FRANÇAIS: A Dual-Language Book, Wallace Fowlie. Ten stories by French masters, Voltaire to Camus: "Micromegas" by Voltaire; "The Atheist's Mass" by Balzac; "Minuet" by de Maupassant; "The Guest" by Camus, six more. Excellent English translations on facing pages. Also French-English vocabulary list, exercises, more. 352pp. 5⅜ x 8½. 26443-2

CHICAGO AT THE TURN OF THE CENTURY IN PHOTOGRAPHS: 122 Historic Views from the Collections of the Chicago Historical Society, Larry A. Viskochil. Rare large-format prints offer detailed views of City Hall, State Street, the Loop, Hull House, Union Station, many other landmarks, circa 1904-1913. Introduction. Captions. Maps. 144pp. 9⅜ x 12¼. 24656-6

OLD BROOKLYN IN EARLY PHOTOGRAPHS, 1865-1929, William Lee Younger. Luna Park, Gravesend race track, construction of Grand Army Plaza, moving of Hotel Brighton, etc. 157 previously unpublished photographs. 165pp. 8⅞ x 11¾. 23587-4

THE MYTHS OF THE NORTH AMERICAN INDIANS, Lewis Spence. Rich anthology of the myths and legends of the Algonquins, Iroquois, Pawnees and Sioux, prefaced by an extensive historical and ethnological commentary. 36 illustrations. 480pp. 5⅜ x 8½. 25967-6

AN ENCYCLOPEDIA OF BATTLES: Accounts of Over 1,560 Battles from 1479 B.C. to the Present, David Eggenberger. Essential details of every major battle in recorded history from the first battle of Megiddo in 1479 B.C. to Grenada in 1984. List of Battle Maps. New Appendix covering the years 1967-1984. Index. 99 illustrations. 544pp. 6½ x 9¼. 24913-1

SAILING ALONE AROUND THE WORLD, Captain Joshua Slocum. First man to sail around the world, alone, in small boat. One of great feats of seamanship told in delightful manner. 67 illustrations. 294pp. 5⅜ x 8½. 20326-3

ANARCHISM AND OTHER ESSAYS, Emma Goldman. Powerful, penetrating, prophetic essays on direct action, role of minorities, prison reform, puritan hypocrisy, violence, etc. 271pp. 5⅜ x 8½. 22484-8

MYTHS OF THE HINDUS AND BUDDHISTS, Ananda K. Coomaraswamy and Sister Nivedita. Great stories of the epics; deeds of Krishna, Shiva, taken from puranas, Vedas, folk tales; etc. 32 illustrations. 400pp. 5⅜ x 8½. 21759-0

THE TRAUMA OF BIRTH, Otto Rank. Rank's controversial thesis that anxiety neurosis is caused by profound psychological trauma which occurs at birth. 256pp. 5⅜ x 8½. 27974-X

A THEOLOGICO-POLITICAL TREATISE, Benedict Spinoza. Also contains unfinished Political Treatise. Great classic on religious liberty, theory of government on common consent. R. Elwes translation. Total of 421pp. 5⅜ x 8½. 20249-6

MY BONDAGE AND MY FREEDOM, Frederick Douglass. Born a slave, Douglass became outspoken force in antislavery movement. The best of Douglass' autobiographies. Graphic description of slave life. 464pp. 5⅜ x 8½.　　22457-0

FOLLOWING THE EQUATOR: A Journey Around the World, Mark Twain. Fascinating humorous account of 1897 voyage to Hawaii, Australia, India, New Zealand, etc. Ironic, bemused reports on peoples, customs, climate, flora and fauna, politics, much more. 197 illustrations. 720pp. 5⅜ x 8½.　　26113-1

THE PEOPLE CALLED SHAKERS, Edward D. Andrews. Definitive study of Shakers: origins, beliefs, practices, dances, social organization, furniture and crafts, etc. 33 illustrations. 351pp. 5⅜ x 8½.　　21081-2

THE MYTHS OF GREECE AND ROME, H. A. Guerber. A classic of mythology, generously illustrated, long prized for its simple, graphic, accurate retelling of the principal myths of Greece and Rome, and for its commentary on their origins and significance. With 64 illustrations by Michelangelo, Raphael, Titian, Rubens, Canova, Bernini and others. 480pp. 5⅜ x 8½.　　27584-1

PSYCHOLOGY OF MUSIC, Carl E. Seashore. Classic work discusses music as a medium from psychological viewpoint. Clear treatment of physical acoustics, auditory apparatus, sound perception, development of musical skills, nature of musical feeling, host of other topics. 88 figures. 408pp. 5⅜ x 8½.　　21851-1

THE PHILOSOPHY OF HISTORY, Georg W. Hegel. Great classic of Western thought develops concept that history is not chance but rational process, the evolution of freedom. 457pp. 5⅜ x 8½.　　20112-0

THE BOOK OF TEA, Kakuzo Okakura. Minor classic of the Orient: entertaining, charming explanation, interpretation of traditional Japanese culture in terms of tea ceremony. 94pp. 5⅜ x 8½.　　20070-1

LIFE IN ANCIENT EGYPT, Adolf Erman. Fullest, most thorough, detailed older account with much not in more recent books, domestic life, religion, magic, medicine, commerce, much more. Many illustrations reproduce tomb paintings, carvings, hieroglyphs, etc. 597pp. 5⅜ x 8½.　　22632-8

SUNDIALS, Their Theory and Construction, Albert Waugh. Far and away the best, most thorough coverage of ideas, mathematics concerned, types, construction, adjusting anywhere. Simple, nontechnical treatment allows even children to build several of these dials. Over 100 illustrations. 230pp. 5⅜ x 8½.　　22947-5

THEORETICAL HYDRODYNAMICS, L. M. Milne-Thomson. Classic exposition of the mathematical theory of fluid motion, applicable to both hydrodynamics and aerodynamics. Over 600 exercises. 768pp. 6⅛ x 9¼.　　68970-0

SONGS OF EXPERIENCE: Facsimile Reproduction with 26 Plates in Full Color, William Blake. 26 full-color plates from a rare 1826 edition. Includes "The Tyger," "London," "Holy Thursday," and other poems. Printed text of poems. 48pp. 5¼ x 7.　　24636-1

OLD-TIME VIGNETTES IN FULL COLOR, Carol Belanger Grafton (ed.). Over 390 charming, often sentimental illustrations, selected from archives of Victorian graphics—pretty women posing, children playing, food, flowers, kittens and puppies, smiling cherubs, birds and butterflies, much more. All copyright-free. 48pp. 9¼ x 12¼.　　27269-9

PERSPECTIVE FOR ARTISTS, Rex Vicat Cole. Depth, perspective of sky and sea, shadows, much more, not usually covered. 391 diagrams, 81 reproductions of drawings and paintings. 279pp. 5⅜ x 8½. 22487-2

DRAWING THE LIVING FIGURE, Joseph Sheppard. Innovative approach to artistic anatomy focuses on specifics of surface anatomy, rather than muscles and bones. Over 170 drawings of live models in front, back and side views, and in widely varying poses. Accompanying diagrams. 177 illustrations. Introduction. Index. 144pp. 8⅜ x11¼. 26723-7

GOTHIC AND OLD ENGLISH ALPHABETS: 100 Complete Fonts, Dan X. Solo. Add power, elegance to posters, signs, other graphics with 100 stunning copyright-free alphabets: Blackstone, Dolbey, Germania, 97 more–including many lower-case, numerals, punctuation marks. 104pp. 8⅛ x 11. 24695-7

HOW TO DO BEADWORK, Mary White. Fundamental book on craft from simple projects to five-bead chains and woven works. 106 illustrations. 142pp. 5⅜ x 8. 20697-1

THE BOOK OF WOOD CARVING, Charles Marshall Sayers. Finest book for beginners discusses fundamentals and offers 34 designs. "Absolutely first rate . . . well thought out and well executed."–E. J. Tangerman. 118pp. 7¾ x 10⅝. 23654-4

ILLUSTRATED CATALOG OF CIVIL WAR MILITARY GOODS: Union Army Weapons, Insignia, Uniform Accessories, and Other Equipment, Schuyler, Hartley, and Graham. Rare, profusely illustrated 1846 catalog includes Union Army uniform and dress regulations, arms and ammunition, coats, insignia, flags, swords, rifles, etc. 226 illustrations. 160pp. 9 x 12. 24939-5

WOMEN'S FASHIONS OF THE EARLY 1900s: An Unabridged Republication of "New York Fashions, 1909," National Cloak & Suit Co. Rare catalog of mail-order fashions documents women's and children's clothing styles shortly after the turn of the century. Captions offer full descriptions, prices. Invaluable resource for fashion, costume historians. Approximately 725 illustrations. 128pp. 8⅜ x 11¼. 27276-1

THE 1912 AND 1915 GUSTAV STICKLEY FURNITURE CATALOGS, Gustav Stickley. With over 200 detailed illustrations and descriptions, these two catalogs are essential reading and reference materials and identification guides for Stickley furniture. Captions cite materials, dimensions and prices. 112pp. 6½ x 9¼. 26676-1

EARLY AMERICAN LOCOMOTIVES, John H. White, Jr. Finest locomotive engravings from early 19th century: historical (1804–74), main-line (after 1870), special, foreign, etc. 147 plates. 142pp. 11⅜ x 8¼. 22772-3

THE TALL SHIPS OF TODAY IN PHOTOGRAPHS, Frank O. Braynard. Lavishly illustrated tribute to nearly 100 majestic contemporary sailing vessels: Amerigo Vespucci, Clearwater, Constitution, Eagle, Mayflower, Sea Cloud, Victory, many more. Authoritative captions provide statistics, background on each ship. 190 black-and-white photographs and illustrations. Introduction. 128pp. 8⅞ x 11¾. 27163-3

LITTLE BOOK OF EARLY AMERICAN CRAFTS AND TRADES, Peter Stockham (ed.). 1807 children's book explains crafts and trades: baker, hatter, cooper, potter, and many others. 23 copperplate illustrations. 140pp. 4⅝ x 6.   23336-7

VICTORIAN FASHIONS AND COSTUMES FROM HARPER'S BAZAR, 1867–1898, Stella Blum (ed.). Day costumes, evening wear, sports clothes, shoes, hats, other accessories in over 1,000 detailed engravings. 320pp. 9⅜ x 12¼. 22990-4

GUSTAV STICKLEY, THE CRAFTSMAN, Mary Ann Smith. Superb study surveys broad scope of Stickley's achievement, especially in architecture. Design philosophy, rise and fall of the Craftsman empire, descriptions and floor plans for many Craftsman houses, more. 86 black-and-white halftones. 31 line illustrations. Introduction 208pp. 6½ x 9¼.   27210-9

THE LONG ISLAND RAIL ROAD IN EARLY PHOTOGRAPHS, Ron Ziel. Over 220 rare photos, informative text document origin (1844) and development of rail service on Long Island. Vintage views of early trains, locomotives, stations, passengers, crews, much more. Captions. 8⅞ x 11¾.   26301-0

VOYAGE OF THE LIBERDADE, Joshua Slocum. Great 19th-century mariner's thrilling, first-hand account of the wreck of his ship off South America, the 35-foot boat he built from the wreckage, and its remarkable voyage home. 128pp. 5⅜ x 8½.
40022-0

TEN BOOKS ON ARCHITECTURE, Vitruvius. The most important book ever written on architecture. Early Roman aesthetics, technology, classical orders, site selection, all other aspects. Morgan translation. 331pp. 5⅜ x 8½.   20645-9

THE HUMAN FIGURE IN MOTION, Eadweard Muybridge. More than 4,500 stopped-action photos, in action series, showing undraped men, women, children jumping, lying down, throwing, sitting, wrestling, carrying, etc. 390pp. 7⅞ x 10⅝.
20204-6 Clothbd.

TREES OF THE EASTERN AND CENTRAL UNITED STATES AND CANADA, William M. Harlow. Best one-volume guide to 140 trees. Full descriptions, woodlore, range, etc. Over 600 illustrations. Handy size. 288pp. 4½ x 6⅜.   20395-6

SONGS OF WESTERN BIRDS, Dr. Donald J. Borror. Complete song and call repertoire of 60 western species, including flycatchers, juncoes, cactus wrens, many more—includes fully illustrated booklet.   Cassette and manual 99913-0

GROWING AND USING HERBS AND SPICES, Milo Miloradovich. Versatile handbook provides all the information needed for cultivation and use of all the herbs and spices available in North America. 4 illustrations. Index. Glossary. 236pp. 5⅜ x 8½.
25058-X

BIG BOOK OF MAZES AND LABYRINTHS, Walter Shepherd. 50 mazes and labyrinths in all—classical, solid, ripple, and more—in one great volume. Perfect inexpensive puzzler for clever youngsters. Full solutions. 112pp. 8⅛ x 11.   22951-3

PIANO TUNING, J. Cree Fischer. Clearest, best book for beginner, amateur. Simple repairs, raising dropped notes, tuning by easy method of flattened fifths. No previous skills needed. 4 illustrations. 201pp. 5⅜ x 8½. 23267-0

HINTS TO SINGERS, Lillian Nordica. Selecting the right teacher, developing confidence, overcoming stage fright, and many other important skills receive thoughtful discussion in this indispensible guide, written by a world-famous diva of four decades' experience. 96pp. 5⅜ x 8½. 40094-8

THE COMPLETE NONSENSE OF EDWARD LEAR, Edward Lear. All nonsense limericks, zany alphabets, Owl and Pussycat, songs, nonsense botany, etc., illustrated by Lear. Total of 320pp. 5⅜ x 8½. (Available in U.S. only.) 20167-8

VICTORIAN PARLOUR POETRY: An Annotated Anthology, Michael R. Turner. 117 gems by Longfellow, Tennyson, Browning, many lesser-known poets. "The Village Blacksmith," "Curfew Must Not Ring Tonight," "Only a Baby Small," dozens more, often difficult to find elsewhere. Index of poets, titles, first lines. xxiii + 325pp. 5⅜ x 8¼. 27044-0

DUBLINERS, James Joyce. Fifteen stories offer vivid, tightly focused observations of the lives of Dublin's poorer classes. At least one, "The Dead," is considered a masterpiece. Reprinted complete and unabridged from standard edition. 160pp. 5³⁄₁₆ x 8¼. 26870-5

GREAT WEIRD TALES: 14 Stories by Lovecraft, Blackwood, Machen and Others, S. T. Joshi (ed.). 14 spellbinding tales, including "The Sin Eater," by Fiona McLeod, "The Eye Above the Mantel," by Frank Belknap Long, as well as renowned works by R. H. Barlow, Lord Dunsany, Arthur Machen, W. C. Morrow and eight other masters of the genre. 256pp. 5⅜ x 8½. (Available in U.S. only.) 40436-6

THE BOOK OF THE SACRED MAGIC OF ABRAMELIN THE MAGE, translated by S. MacGregor Mathers. Medieval manuscript of ceremonial magic. Basic document in Aleister Crowley, Golden Dawn groups. 268pp. 5⅜ x 8½. 23211-5

NEW RUSSIAN-ENGLISH AND ENGLISH-RUSSIAN DICTIONARY, M. A. O'Brien. This is a remarkably handy Russian dictionary, containing a surprising amount of information, including over 70,000 entries. 366pp. 4½ x 6⅛. 20208-9

HISTORIC HOMES OF THE AMERICAN PRESIDENTS, Second, Revised Edition, Irvin Haas. A traveler's guide to American Presidential homes, most open to the public, depicting and describing homes occupied by every American President from George Washington to George Bush. With visiting hours, admission charges, travel routes. 175 photographs. Index. 160pp. 8¼ x 11. 26751-2

NEW YORK IN THE FORTIES, Andreas Feininger. 162 brilliant photographs by the well-known photographer, formerly with *Life* magazine. Commuters, shoppers, Times Square at night, much else from city at its peak. Captions by John von Hartz. 181pp. 9¼ x 10¾. 23585-8

INDIAN SIGN LANGUAGE, William Tomkins. Over 525 signs developed by Sioux and other tribes. Written instructions and diagrams. Also 290 pictographs. 111pp. 6⅛ x 9¼. 22029-X

CATALOG OF DOVER BOOKS

ANATOMY: A Complete Guide for Artists, Joseph Sheppard. A master of figure drawing shows artists how to render human anatomy convincingly. Over 460 illustrations. 224pp. 8⅜ x 11¼.   27279-6

MEDIEVAL CALLIGRAPHY: Its History and Technique, Marc Drogin. Spirited history, comprehensive instruction manual covers 13 styles (ca. 4th century through 15th). Excellent photographs; directions for duplicating medieval techniques with modern tools. 224pp. 8⅜ x 11¼.   26142-5

DRIED FLOWERS: How to Prepare Them, Sarah Whitlock and Martha Rankin. Complete instructions on how to use silica gel, meal and borax, perlite aggregate, sand and borax, glycerine and water to create attractive permanent flower arrangements. 12 illustrations. 32pp. 5⅜ x 8½.   21802-3

EASY-TO-MAKE BIRD FEEDERS FOR WOODWORKERS, Scott D. Campbell. Detailed, simple-to-use guide for designing, constructing, caring for and using feeders. Text, illustrations for 12 classic and contemporary designs. 96pp. 5⅜ x 8½.
                                                                            25847-5

SCOTTISH WONDER TALES FROM MYTH AND LEGEND, Donald A. Mackenzie. 16 lively tales tell of giants rumbling down mountainsides, of a magic wand that turns stone pillars into warriors, of gods and goddesses, evil hags, powerful forces and more. 240pp. 5⅜ x 8½.   29677-6

THE HISTORY OF UNDERCLOTHES, C. Willett Cunnington and Phyllis Cunnington. Fascinating, well-documented survey covering six centuries of English undergarments, enhanced with over 100 illustrations: 12th-century laced-up bodice, footed long drawers (1795), 19th-century bustles, l9th-century corsets for men, Victorian "bust improvers," much more. 272pp. 5⅜ x 8¼.   27124-2

ARTS AND CRAFTS FURNITURE: The Complete Brooks Catalog of 1912, Brooks Manufacturing Co. Photos and detailed descriptions of more than 150 now very collectible furniture designs from the Arts and Crafts movement depict davenports, settees, buffets, desks, tables, chairs, bedsteads, dressers and more, all built of solid, quarter-sawed oak. Invaluable for students and enthusiasts of antiques, Americana and the decorative arts. 80pp. 6½ x 9¼.   27471-3

WILBUR AND ORVILLE: A Biography of the Wright Brothers, Fred Howard. Definitive, crisply written study tells the full story of the brothers' lives and work. A vividly written biography, unparalleled in scope and color, that also captures the spirit of an extraordinary era. 560pp. 6⅛ x 9¼.   40297-5

THE ARTS OF THE SAILOR: Knotting, Splicing and Ropework, Hervey Garrett Smith. Indispensable shipboard reference covers tools, basic knots and useful hitches; handsewing and canvas work, more. Over 100 illustrations. Delightful reading for sea lovers. 256pp. 5⅜ x 8½.   26440-8

FRANK LLOYD WRIGHT'S FALLINGWATER: The House and Its History, Second, Revised Edition, Donald Hoffmann. A total revision—both in text and illustrations—of the standard document on Fallingwater, the boldest, most personal architectural statement of Wright's mature years, updated with valuable new material from the recently opened Frank Lloyd Wright Archives. "Fascinating"—The New York Times. 116 illustrations. 128pp. 9¼ x 10¾.   27430-6

PHOTOGRAPHIC SKETCHBOOK OF THE CIVIL WAR, Alexander Gardner. 100 photos taken on field during the Civil War. Famous shots of Manassas Harper's Ferry, Lincoln, Richmond, slave pens, etc. 244pp. 10⅝ x 8¼. 22731-6

FIVE ACRES AND INDEPENDENCE, Maurice G. Kains. Great back-to-the-land classic explains basics of self-sufficient farming. The one book to get. 95 illustrations. 397pp. 5⅜ x 8½. 20974-1

SONGS OF EASTERN BIRDS, Dr. Donald J. Borror. Songs and calls of 60 species most common to eastern U.S.: warblers, woodpeckers, flycatchers, thrushes, larks, many more in high-quality recording. Cassette and manual 99912-2

A MODERN HERBAL, Margaret Grieve. Much the fullest, most exact, most useful compilation of herbal material. Gigantic alphabetical encyclopedia, from aconite to zedoary, gives botanical information, medical properties, folklore, economic uses, much else. Indispensable to serious reader. 161 illustrations. 888pp. 6½ x 9¼. 2-vol. set. (Available in U.S. only.)
Vol. I: 22798-7
Vol. II: 22799-5

HIDDEN TREASURE MAZE BOOK, Dave Phillips. Solve 34 challenging mazes accompanied by heroic tales of adventure. Evil dragons, people-eating plants, blood-thirsty giants, many more dangerous adversaries lurk at every twist and turn. 34 mazes, stories, solutions. 48pp. 8¼ x 11. 24566-7

LETTERS OF W. A. MOZART, Wolfgang A. Mozart. Remarkable letters show bawdy wit, humor, imagination, musical insights, contemporary musical world; includes some letters from Leopold Mozart. 276pp. 5⅜ x 8½. 22859-2

BASIC PRINCIPLES OF CLASSICAL BALLET, Agrippina Vaganova. Great Russian theoretician, teacher explains methods for teaching classical ballet. 118 illustrations. 175pp. 5⅜ x 8½. 22036-2

THE JUMPING FROG, Mark Twain. Revenge edition. The original story of The Celebrated Jumping Frog of Calaveras County, a hapless French translation, and Twain's hilarious "retranslation" from the French. 12 illustrations. 66pp. 5⅜ x 8½. 22686-7

BEST REMEMBERED POEMS, Martin Gardner (ed.). The 126 poems in this superb collection of 19th- and 20th-century British and American verse range from Shelley's "To a Skylark" to the impassioned "Renascence" of Edna St. Vincent Millay and to Edward Lear's whimsical "The Owl and the Pussycat." 224pp. 5⅜ x 8½. 27165-X

COMPLETE SONNETS, William Shakespeare. Over 150 exquisite poems deal with love, friendship, the tyranny of time, beauty's evanescence, death and other themes in language of remarkable power, precision and beauty. Glossary of archaic terms. 80pp. 5³⁄₁₆ x 8¼. 26686-9

THE BATTLES THAT CHANGED HISTORY, Fletcher Pratt. Eminent historian profiles 16 crucial conflicts, ancient to modern, that changed the course of civilization. 352pp. 5⅜ x 8½. 41129-X

THE WIT AND HUMOR OF OSCAR WILDE, Alvin Redman (ed.). More than 1,000 ripostes, paradoxes, wisecracks: Work is the curse of the drinking classes; I can resist everything except temptation; etc. 258pp. 5⅜ x 8½. 20602-5

SHAKESPEARE LEXICON AND QUOTATION DICTIONARY, Alexander Schmidt. Full definitions, locations, shades of meaning in every word in plays and poems. More than 50,000 exact quotations. 1,485pp. 6½ x 9¼. 2-vol. set.
Vol. 1: 22726-X
Vol. 2: 22727-8

SELECTED POEMS, Emily Dickinson. Over 100 best-known, best-loved poems by one of America's foremost poets, reprinted from authoritative early editions. No comparable edition at this price. Index of first lines. 64pp. 5³⁄₁₆ x 8¼. 26466-1

THE INSIDIOUS DR. FU-MANCHU, Sax Rohmer. The first of the popular mystery series introduces a pair of English detectives to their archnemesis, the diabolical Dr. Fu-Manchu. Flavorful atmosphere, fast-paced action, and colorful characters enliven this classic of the genre. 208pp. 5³⁄₁₆ x 8¼. 29898-1

THE MALLEUS MALEFICARUM OF KRAMER AND SPRENGER, translated by Montague Summers. Full text of most important witchhunter's "bible," used by both Catholics and Protestants. 278pp. 6⅝ x 10. 22802-9

SPANISH STORIES/CUENTOS ESPAÑOLES: A Dual-Language Book, Angel Flores (ed.). Unique format offers 13 great stories in Spanish by Cervantes, Borges, others. Faithful English translations on facing pages. 352pp. 5⅜ x 8½. 25399-6

GARDEN CITY, LONG ISLAND, IN EARLY PHOTOGRAPHS, 1869–1919, Mildred H. Smith. Handsome treasury of 118 vintage pictures, accompanied by carefully researched captions, document the Garden City Hotel fire (1899), the Vanderbilt Cup Race (1908), the first airmail flight departing from the Nassau Boulevard Aerodrome (1911), and much more. 96pp. 8⅞ x 11¾. 40669-5

OLD QUEENS, N.Y., IN EARLY PHOTOGRAPHS, Vincent F. Seyfried and William Asadorian. Over 160 rare photographs of Maspeth, Jamaica, Jackson Heights, and other areas. Vintage views of DeWitt Clinton mansion, 1939 World's Fair and more. Captions. 192pp. 8⅞ x 11. 26358-4

CAPTURED BY THE INDIANS: 15 Firsthand Accounts, 1750-1870, Frederick Drimmer. Astounding true historical accounts of grisly torture, bloody conflicts, relentless pursuits, miraculous escapes and more, by people who lived to tell the tale. 384pp. 5⅜ x 8½. 24901-8

THE WORLD'S GREAT SPEECHES (Fourth Enlarged Edition), Lewis Copeland, Lawrence W. Lamm, and Stephen J. McKenna. Nearly 300 speeches provide public speakers with a wealth of updated quotes and inspiration–from Pericles' funeral oration and William Jennings Bryan's "Cross of Gold Speech" to Malcolm X's powerful words on the Black Revolution and Earl of Spenser's tribute to his sister, Diana, Princess of Wales. 944pp. 5⅜ x 8⅜. 40903-1

THE BOOK OF THE SWORD, Sir Richard F. Burton. Great Victorian scholar/adventurer's eloquent, erudite history of the "queen of weapons"–from prehistory to early Roman Empire. Evolution and development of early swords, variations (sabre, broadsword, cutlass, scimitar, etc.), much more. 336pp. 6⅛ x 9¼.
25434-8

AUTOBIOGRAPHY: The Story of My Experiments with Truth, Mohandas K. Gandhi. Boyhood, legal studies, purification, the growth of the Satyagraha (nonviolent protest) movement. Critical, inspiring work of the man responsible for the freedom of India. 480pp. 5⅜ x 8½. (Available in U.S. only.) 24593-4

CELTIC MYTHS AND LEGENDS, T. W. Rolleston. Masterful retelling of Irish and Welsh stories and tales. Cuchulain, King Arthur, Deirdre, the Grail, many more. First paperback edition. 58 full-page illustrations. 512pp. 5⅜ x 8½. 26507-2

THE PRINCIPLES OF PSYCHOLOGY, William James. Famous long course complete, unabridged. Stream of thought, time perception, memory, experimental methods; great work decades ahead of its time. 94 figures. 1,391pp. 5⅜ x 8½. 2-vol. set.
Vol. I: 20381-6 Vol. II: 20382-4

THE WORLD AS WILL AND REPRESENTATION, Arthur Schopenhauer. Definitive English translation of Schopenhauer's life work, correcting more than 1,000 errors, omissions in earlier translations. Translated by E. F. J. Payne. Total of 1,269pp. 5⅜ x 8½. 2-vol. set. Vol. 1: 21761-2 Vol. 2: 21762-0

MAGIC AND MYSTERY IN TIBET, Madame Alexandra David-Neel. Experiences among lamas, magicians, sages, sorcerers, Bonpa wizards. A true psychic discovery. 32 illustrations. 321pp. 5⅜ x 8½. (Available in U.S. only.) 22682-4

THE EGYPTIAN BOOK OF THE DEAD, E. A. Wallis Budge. Complete reproduction of Ani's papyrus, finest ever found. Full hieroglyphic text, interlinear transliteration, word-for-word translation, smooth translation. 533pp. 6½ x 9¼. 21866-X

MATHEMATICS FOR THE NONMATHEMATICIAN, Morris Kline. Detailed, college-level treatment of mathematics in cultural and historical context, with numerous exercises. Recommended Reading Lists. Tables. Numerous figures. 641pp. 5⅜ x 8½.
24823-2

PROBABILISTIC METHODS IN THE THEORY OF STRUCTURES, Isaac Elishakoff. Well-written introduction covers the elements of the theory of probability from two or more random variables, the reliability of such multivariable structures, the theory of random function, Monte Carlo methods of treating problems incapable of exact solution, and more. Examples. 502pp. 5⅜ x 8½. 40691-1

THE RIME OF THE ANCIENT MARINER, Gustave Doré, S. T. Coleridge. Doré's finest work; 34 plates capture moods, subtleties of poem. Flawless full-size reproductions printed on facing pages with authoritative text of poem. "Beautiful. Simply beautiful."–*Publisher's Weekly*. 77pp. 9¼ x 12. 22305-1

NORTH AMERICAN INDIAN DESIGNS FOR ARTISTS AND CRAFTSPEOPLE, Eva Wilson. Over 360 authentic copyright-free designs adapted from Navajo blankets, Hopi pottery, Sioux buffalo hides, more. Geometrics, symbolic figures, plant and animal motifs, etc. 128pp. 8⅜ x 11. (Not for sale in the United Kingdom.) 25341-4

SCULPTURE: Principles and Practice, Louis Slobodkin. Step-by-step approach to clay, plaster, metals, stone; classical and modern. 253 drawings, photos. 255pp. 8⅛ x 11.
22960-2

THE INFLUENCE OF SEA POWER UPON HISTORY, 1660–1783, A. T. Mahan. Influential classic of naval history and tactics still used as text in war colleges. First paperback edition. 4 maps. 24 battle plans. 640pp. 5⅜ x 8½. 25509-3

THE STORY OF THE TITANIC AS TOLD BY ITS SURVIVORS, Jack Winocour (ed.). What it was really like. Panic, despair, shocking inefficiency, and a little heroism. More thrilling than any fictional account. 26 illustrations. 320pp. 5⅜ x 8½.
20610-6

FAIRY AND FOLK TALES OF THE IRISH PEASANTRY, William Butler Yeats (ed.). Treasury of 64 tales from the twilight world of Celtic myth and legend: "The Soul Cages," "The Kildare Pooka," "King O'Toole and his Goose," many more. Introduction and Notes by W. B. Yeats. 352pp. 5⅜ x 8½.
26941-8

BUDDHIST MAHAYANA TEXTS, E. B. Cowell and others (eds.). Superb, accurate translations of basic documents in Mahayana Buddhism, highly important in history of religions. The Buddha-karita of Asvaghosha, Larger Sukhavativyuha, more. 448pp. 5⅜ x 8½.
25552-2

ONE TWO THREE . . . INFINITY: Facts and Speculations of Science, George Gamow. Great physicist's fascinating, readable overview of contemporary science: number theory, relativity, fourth dimension, entropy, genes, atomic structure, much more. 128 illustrations. Index. 352pp. 5⅜ x 8½.
25664-2

EXPERIMENTATION AND MEASUREMENT, W. J. Youden. Introductory manual explains laws of measurement in simple terms and offers tips for achieving accuracy and minimizing errors. Mathematics of measurement, use of instruments, experimenting with machines. 1994 edition. Foreword. Preface. Introduction. Epilogue. Selected Readings. Glossary. Index. Tables and figures. 128pp. 5⅜ x 8½. 40451-X

DALÍ ON MODERN ART: The Cuckolds of Antiquated Modern Art, Salvador Dalí. Influential painter skewers modern art and its practitioners. Outrageous evaluations of Picasso, Cézanne, Turner, more. 15 renderings of paintings discussed. 44 calligraphic decorations by Dalí. 96pp. 5⅜ x 8½. (Available in U.S. only.) 29220-7

ANTIQUE PLAYING CARDS: A Pictorial History, Henry René D'Allemagne. Over 900 elaborate, decorative images from rare playing cards (14th–20th centuries): Bacchus, death, dancing dogs, hunting scenes, royal coats of arms, players cheating, much more. 96pp. 9¼ x 12¼.
29265-7

MAKING FURNITURE MASTERPIECES: 30 Projects with Measured Drawings, Franklin H. Gottshall. Step-by-step instructions, illustrations for constructing handsome, useful pieces, among them a Sheraton desk, Chippendale chair, Spanish desk, Queen Anne table and a William and Mary dressing mirror. 224pp. 8⅛ x 11¼.
29338-6

THE FOSSIL BOOK: A Record of Prehistoric Life, Patricia V. Rich et al. Profusely illustrated definitive guide covers everything from single-celled organisms and dinosaurs to birds and mammals and the interplay between climate and man. Over 1,500 illustrations. 760pp. 7½ x 10⅛.
29371-8

Paperbound unless otherwise indicated. Available at your book dealer, online at **www.doverpublications.com**, or by writing to Dept. GI, Dover Publications, Inc., 31 East 2nd Street, Mineola, NY 11501. For current price information or for free catalogues (please indicate field of interest), write to Dover Publications or log on to **www.doverpublications.com** and see every Dover book in print. Dover publishes more than 500 books each year on science, elementary and advanced mathematics, biology, music, art, literary history, social sciences, and other areas.